For my parents:

my beloved father,
who I miss every day and
who adored Brazil;

and my wise, kind,
beautiful Brazilian mother—
the inspiration for this
book, who I'd be lost without.

Loving you since always.

FUSÃO

Interlink Books

IXTA BELFRAGE

UNTRADITIONAL
RECIPES INSPIRED
BY *BRASIL*

FUSÃO
Ixta Belfrage

Brazil photography
Pedro Pinho

Brazil production
Romã Nesi Pio

Recipe photography
Kim Lightbody

Recipe set design
Felicity Davis

10	**INTRODUCTION**
20	**INGREDIENTS**
24	**FLAVOR BOMBS**
32	**VEGETABLES**
40	*Minas Gerais*
45	*Heloísa*
60	*Citrus*
84	*Music, Politics, Food*
102	**SEAFOOD**
108	*The Amazon and Kenrick*
124	*Azeite de Dendê*
126	*Silvio*
164	*Jorge Washington*
178	**MEAT**
184	*Middle Eastern Immigration*
194	*Cassava and Tucupi*
212	*Japanese Immigration*
224	*Italian Immigration*
232	**SWEET**
240	*Memories of Family and Food*
280	**INDEX**
286	**THANKS**

FUSÃO (pronounced "foo-zow," with a soft "z" and a nasalized "ow̃" sound) means fusion, or union, in Portuguese, though it's not usually a word associated with food—more so with chemistry or music. It is, however, a beautiful word whose meaning is easily understandable even if you don't speak Portuguese, and I love the idea of giving new meaning to it. After all, language, like food, is ever-evolving.

In the context of this book, the word *fusão* describes me: the union of a Brazilian mother and an English father. It also describes Brazilian cuisine: a fusion of Indigenous, Portuguese and West African influences that incorporates inspiration from diverse immigrant populations. Following on from my last book, MEZCLA, this book is a continuation of the theme of fusion cooking, this time through the lens of Brazil.

The idea for this book came to me after doing a genealogy test, which showed that my Brazilian half comprised a mix of Indigenous, Portuguese and African ancestry. The results were encouragement to delve deeper into that side of my heritage, and in the process of researching this book I've been back to Brazil many times over the last few years. With each visit my feelings become more complex. My love for Brazil runs deep, but I never feel at home there: my Portuguese is shaky, I don't look Brazilian and there are certain nuances that can only be understood when you grow up somewhere. Despite the fact that my Brazilian friends and family welcome me with open arms, I always feel like an imposter.

Food, therefore, has become my bridge to Brazil and a way to connect with that side of my heritage. Much of my research has been informed by a seminal book, *História da Alimentação no Brasil* (*The History of Food in Brazil*), written by Luís da Câmara Cascudo in 1967. It just so happens that Câmara Cascudo was a cousin of my great-grandmother Maria Eugênia, so when the imposter syndrome sets in, I try to remind myself that in a roundabout way, perhaps I'm carrying some sort of Brazilian culinary torch?

Ultimately, though, this book barely scratches the surface of Brazil. Brazil is vast and breathtaking, complex and beautiful. It's a place that defies being fully captured and this book doesn't try to. *FUSÃO* isn't a definitive guide to Brazilian cuisine, rather a deeply personal journey featuring the people I've met along the way and the recipes that this has inspired. In the multiple trips I took to Brazil to do my research, I often chose to go back to the same places to revisit the same people, rather than trying to cover more ground with broad brushstrokes. I'm looking forward to introducing you to these characters—each of whom have shaped my understanding of the world in unexpected ways.

I may never feel entirely at home in Brazil, but exploring the country through the context of food has been a way for me to connect with places and people in a way that feels really profound. A means to bridge the gap between who I am and where my mother is from. FUSÃO explores all of this, offering over eighty vibrant, untraditional recipes inspired by Brazil, with an Ixta twist.

My mom moved to London from Brazil when she was twenty-eight and yet she is unequivocally Brazilian, in the way she speaks, sings, laughs, and in the way she moves through the world. She was born in Botafogo, Rio de Janeiro, in 1958 and lived in Bairro Peixoto, Copacabana, for the first few years of her life. Her parents were both from Natal, the capital of the state of Rio Grande do Norte. At the time, Bairro Peixoto was a haven for left-wing activists, of which my grandfather was one (see page 84 for more on politics and the military dictatorship).

My grandparents moved back to Natal with my mother not long after, and it was in the home of their grandparents that my mother and her siblings have their fondest childhood memories. The beating heart of their home was the kitchen; food was always being prepared. *Feijão* (black beans) is a staple in every Brazilian household and each morning my mother would wake to the smell of *feijão* and *refogado* (a sofrito made of onions, garlic, herbs and spices used to flavor beans) bubbling away. Breakfast consisted of *tapioca* (pancakes made from cassava starch) filled with eggs, cheese and *manteiga de garrafa* (clarified butter, literally "bottle butter," so-called because of its liquid state) and tropical fruits like *mamão, manga, carambola, maracujá, abacaxi, goiaba* (papaya, mango, star fruit, passion fruit, pineapple, guava).

In those days, fishermen would come straight to your door to sell their morning catch. Dairy farmers would bring their cows to the end of the sandy street and you would meet them with a bucket into which they would milk the cows as you waited. From this milk, in all its deliciously raw and unpasteurised glory, my great-grandmother Iracema would make butter and cream, saving the *nata*—the thicker top of the cream and her special treat—to spoon over her *feijão*.

Introduction

There's a misconception that Brazilian food is boring—"It's just rice and beans, right?" is something I've heard people say countless times. This is such a one-dimensional way to describe a country that encompasses 8.51 million square kilometers (3,285,729 square miles), that comprises twenty-six states all with extremely varied cuisines due to terrain, landscape, proximity to bodies of water and to other countries (Brazil borders French Guiana, Suriname, Guyana, Venezuela, Colombia, Peru, Bolivia, Paraguay, Argentina and Uruguay).

"Just rice and beans" greatly oversimplifies the complex history of Brazilian cuisine, which is a mix of Indigenous, Portuguese and African influences.

Take the classic Brazilian dish *moqueca*, a stew made by frying onions, bell peppers and tomatoes in red palm oil, then adding coconut milk and seafood. Many consider *moqueca* to be a classic Brazilian dish, but what that really means is that it's a *fusão*.

Said to have originated with Indigenous Tupi Brazilians, "*moquém*" in Tupi-Guarani language means "a high grill where fish roasts." This earliest version of the dish was adapted with the arrival of Portuguese colonists, who brought with them their tradition of stews. It was then enhanced by enslaved African people (*mu'keka'* in Kimbundu Angolan dialect means "fish stew") who imbued Brazilian cuisine with African soul. The ultimate version of the dish—*moqueca Baiana*—is epitomized by the inclusion of *dendê* (red palm oil) and coconut, which were also taken from their native Africa by Portuguese colonists (see pages 20 and 21).

As if Indigenous, African and Portuguese influences weren't enough, Brazilian cuisine also incorporates inspiration from many other immigrant populations. Migration during the industrialization of the nineteenth and twentieth centuries means that Brazil is now home to huge populations of Italians, Lebanese, Syrians, Palestinians, Japanese, Peruvians, Germans, Hungarians, Poles and Ukrainians, and all these cuisines play a major role in modern Brazilian cuisine.

Lebanese, Syrian and Palestinian people began emigrating to Brazil in the late 1890s, fleeing the political and economic instability caused by the fall of the Ottoman Empire. I expand on the extensive influence of Middle Eastern cuisine on page 184.

I touch upon the influence of Italians, who began emigrating in the 1870s to colonies that had been created to increase Brazil's population, on page 224, and upon the influence of Japanese immigrants, who arrived in the early 1900s as contract agricultural workers, on page 212.

Brazil is a melting pot in the truest sense of the phrase, its cuisine a reflection of a multifaceted, multicultural history as well as of the diversity of its ecosystems.

The characters you'll meet throughout this book reflect this tapestry of diversity: Heloísa is from the state of Minas Gerais, of Turkish descent, Kenrick is from the state of Roraima, of mixed Indigenous and Guyanese descent, Jorge and Silvio are from the state of Bahia, of African descent.

The recipes throughout this book are inspired by this *fusão* of cuisines and cultures, mixed together with the flavors of my upbringing surrounded by Brazilian, Italian and Mexican ingredients and enriched by five years of experience at the Ottolenghi Test Kitchen.

ABOUT THIS BOOK

While it reflects on Brazilian culinary traditions, this is not strictly a book of traditional Brazilian recipes. If you're looking for this, I'd suggest *Travel to Brazil: The Cookbook* by Polyana F. de Oliveira or *Brazilian Food* by Thiago Castanho.

In this book, you'll find twists on classic recipes that will probably make purists uncomfortable. You'll also find new recipes inspired by Brazil, its native ingredients or ingredients that have made their way to Brazilian soil.

If you're Brazilian, you might find yourself flipping through the pages thinking, *This is not how my vovó makes xxx,* and you'd be absolutely right! None of these recipes are strictly traditional and those that are inspired by classics have been adapted with my own personal touch. It's a controversial opinion but I believe there's no "right" way to cook anything. Recipes exist because of innovation, creativity and often because of mistakes, and this is what makes the kitchen an exciting place to be. So trust the process: I've tested these recipes thoroughly and while they may differ from the usual approach, I promise the results will be delicious.

Having said that, I don't need you to follow these recipes to a tee, in fact, I'd prefer if they served as inspiration for you to create your own flavor combinations. You'll notice the recipe section starts with a selection of Flavor Bombs (pages 24–31)—marinades, pickles, oils, sauces—for this very reason. I encourage you to spend a few hours stocking your fridge with these. They'll help ramp up the simplest of meals and will serve as building blocks for you to come up with your own ideas.

The book is simply divided into Flavor Bombs, Vegetables, Seafood, Meat and Sweet. To help you navigate the chapters and decide what you want to cook, I've added timings throughout as well as dietary information, such as whether the recipe is vegan, gluten free or dairy free. I include alternatives and substitutions for Brazilian ingredients on pages 20–23, so you can recreate dishes in kitchens across the world.

THE WAY I COOK, THE INGREDIENTS I USE AND WHY

I won't claim that this is a totally healthy cookbook, but it's probably healthier than most. A large proportion of the recipes are free from gluten, refined sugar, refined oils, grains and dairy (when I refer to dairy here I mean milk, cream and heavy cheeses—I use ghee, butter and yogurt freely).

This reflects how I live my life these days. Around 80% of the time I eat mainly meat, fish, vegetables, fermented foods and complex carbs, and the remaining 20% of the time I eat what I want—usually when I'm out at restaurants. You may think this is irrelevant but it's very important to me and explains the way I cook. Here's some context.

I grew up in a very health-conscious household. My mom has been a nutritionist and functional medicine practitioner since 2003. She got into the field because she had severe health issues growing up and it was only after discovering functional medicine that she was able to heal herself. This journey shaped my upbringing— I wasn't allowed chips, sugar, sodas, gluten, pre-made meals, etc. I used to think this was a gross injustice and I would argue with her, throw tantrums and even steal money to buy candy. Her insistence that I could only eat the foods I begged for if I made them myself was what got me into cooking in the first place.

As a child and young adult, I rebelled against what I knew, as we often do. I buried my head in the sand, but deep down I knew I was food-sensitive and had a lot of the same issues as my mom. I struggled with health problems that only got worse when I started working in the food industry. Insomnia, depression, fatigue, severe digestive issues and constant colds became the norm, until one day, I'd had enough. . .

Fast-forward a few years and I feel better than ever before, because I started listening to my body and eliminating the things that consistently made me unwell. I started developing recipes based on what I could eat, not what I thought people wanted.

This transition happened about halfway through writing this book, so you'll find that many of the recipes reflect my personal food preferences and the way I was raised. You'll find a lot of coconut instead of cream, you'll come across plenty of ghee, you'll notice hardly any gluten or grains, you'll see that I avoid refined oils. You'll notice that I tend to use maple syrup or honey instead of refined sugar. That said, there are some recipes that break these rules, because there's always a time for indulgence and balance is key (although my definition of balance is probably quite different to others').

As my career as a recipe developer evolves, I find myself being drawn more and more to foods that promote healing, because I recognize how much they've changed my life. I relish the challenge of creating healthy recipes that taste incredible. This book marks the beginning of that journey.

I want to caveat all of this by acknowledging that we're all different, and what works for me might not work for you—and vice versa. The last thing I want is to come across as preachy or self-righteous, but I do feel it's important to share the reasoning behind my approach to recipe development and why I tend to favor certain ingredients over others.

INGREDIENTS

This is by no means an exhaustive list of Brazilian ingredients, rather a description of those mentioned throughout the book. I've included substitutions for hard-to-find ingredients as well as Brazilian–Portuguese pronunciations to help you pick up the language!

Azeite de dendê—Red palm oil
≈ ah-zey-chee dje den-deh

Unrefined oil extracted from the fruit of the African oil palm, which was taken to Brazil by Portuguese colonizers during the transatlantic slave trade. *Azeite de dendê* has a deep orange color due to the presence of carotenoids and is used in Afro-Brazilian dishes like *moqueca*, *pirão* and *acarajé* (pages 120, 169 and 98).

Also known as: red oil/palm oil in West African and Caribbean cuisine.
Where to buy: Brazilian, Caribbean and African grocery stores, some supermarkets, online.
Brands I like: Amanprana, Pure Indian Foods, KTC, Juka's Organic Co, Real Food Source.
Substitution: ghee or coconut oil + a little bit of sweet paprika for color (avoid smoked paprika).

Banana da terra—Plantain
≈ bah-nah-na da teh-ha

Literally "banana from the earth." Native to South East Asia, plantain is a large, starchy type of banana that needs to be cooked before eating. All recipes in the book call for ripe plantain. By this I mean that the plantain should be dark yellow in parts but almost completely covered with black marks. It should be slightly soft but not mushy.

Where to buy: Caribbean and African stores, some grocery stores and supermarkets.
Substitution: banana.

Cachaça
≈ kah-shah-sah

The Brazilian national spirit, used to make *caipirinhas*, distilled from fermented sugar-cane juice.

Where to buy: liquor stores, some supermarkets, online.
Brands I like: Abelha, Yaguara, Velho Barreiro.
Substitution: mezcal, tequila, rum.

Camarão seco—Dried shrimp
≈ kah-mah-rown seh-koh

The concentrated flavor of dried shrimp is used to enhance depth and umami in Afro-Brazilian dishes like *maxixada*, *vatapá* and *acarajé*.

Where to buy: Brazilian, Caribbean and African grocery stores, some supermarkets, online.
Substitution: dried anchovies, canned anchovies.

Farinha de mandioca—Coarse cassava flour
≈ fah-reen-yah dje man-dyoh-kah

A coarse flour with the texture of fine breadcrumbs, made from dried cassava. Used as a thickener for soups and stews and to make *farofa*—a textural side dish made with toasted *farinha* fried with ingredients like onion, garlic, egg, bacon, dried shrimp, banana.

Also known as: gari/garri in West African and Caribbean cuisine.
Where to buy: Brazilian, Caribbean and African grocery stores, some supermarkets, online.
Substitution: polenta or cornmeal.

Feijão preto—Black turtle beans
≈ fey-zhau preh-tou

Black beans are a staple across the country. Most Brazilians eat *feijão* every day and especially on Sundays, when they form the base of *feijoada*, a black bean and pork stew served with rice, *farofa*, *couve* and orange slices.

It's important to soak black beans overnight so that they cook evenly. My mom always adds seaweed and a hunk of fresh ginger when soaking; together they act as natural tenderizers, enhance nutritional value and make the beans easier to digest (see page 88).

Where to buy: Brazilian and Latin American grocery stores, most supermarkets.

Folhas de bananeira—Banana leaves
≈ *foh-lyas dje bah-nah-nay-rah*

Banana leaves are used to wrap *abará* and *pamonha* before steaming in north-eastern cuisine, and to wrap fish and meat before grilling in Amazonian cuisine; they add a subtle, earthy flavor.

Wipe the leaves clean on both sides before using, and start with the shiny side down and the matt side up when filling them.

Where to buy: Asian, Latin American or Brazilian grocery stores.
Substitution: corn husks, parchment paper.

Goiaba—Guava
≈ *goh-yah-bah*

A tangy fruit with a pink flesh and an intoxicating aroma that smells sort of like a cross between strawberry and pear. One of the most well-loved iterations of guava in Brazil is *goiabada,* a thick, jelly-like paste made from the pulp and used in desserts, or paired with cheese in a combination called *Romeu e Julieta*.

It can be hard to get guava internationally, so to make guava jam I use a combination of guava juice/purée and ripe strawberries to give body. Try to get pure guava juice or purée without fake flavorings.

Substitution: see above.

Jambu—Pará cress
≈ *zham-boo*

Jambu is a herb native to the Amazon that has a flavor and numbing sensation similar to Szechuan pepper. It's used in dishes like *pato no tucupi* and *tacacá* and to make *cachaça de jambu*. Due to its antimicrobial and anti-inflammatory properties, *jambu* is also used to relieve toothache and reduce inflammation.

Substitution: watercress + a sprinkle of crushed Szechuan pepper.

Leite de coco—Coconut milk
≈ *lay-chee djee koh-koo*

Coconut is another ingredient taken from Africa during the translantic slave trade, which is now ubiquitous in Brazilian cuisine. Coconut milk is essentially just a combination of mature coconut flesh and water. To make your own, put the shredded flesh of 1 mature coconut (6 oz/180 g) into a blender with about 3 cups (700 g) of warm water and blend very well, then strain. Keep refrigerated for up to a week.

When buying canned coconut milk, make sure it's full-fat. Check the ingredient list to make sure it contains at least 70% coconut extract and preferably no oils, gums or thickeners. Coconut milk tends to set hard in cooler weather, in which case whisk it very well before measuring it out for a recipe.

Brands I like: Coconut Merchant, Aroy-D, Tropical Sun, Niru.

Limão cravo
≈ *lee-mawnh krah-voo*

A type of lime (literally lime clove) that grows wild in Brazil and tastes like a cross between a lime and a tangerine but without the sweetness (see page 60).

Substitution: lime + tangerine.

Macaxeira—Cassava
≈ *mah-kah-shey-rah*

A starchy white root vegetable with a thick brown skin native to South America. Known throughout Brazil by different names including *macaxeira, mandioca* and *aipim*—more on page 194. Typically boiled and then mashed or fried, or processed into starch (*tapioca*), flour (*farinha*) or *tucupi*. Also grated and used in desserts like *bolo de macaxeira* (see my version on page 262).

To prepare cassava for recipes in this book, peel away the thick brown skin as well as the pinkish layer beneath. Remove any soft or blackened parts. Cut into 2½ in (6 cm) long cylinders, then halve lengthways. Remove the hard fiber running through the middle, either by pulling it out or with a knife. Put into a bowl of water as you go to prevent discoloration.

Where to buy: Brazilian, Caribbean and African grocery stores, some supermarkets.
Substitution: golden sweet potato, parsnip, yam.

Ingredients

Mamão—Papaya
≈ mah-mownh

Native to central America, papaya was brought to Brazil by Portuguese colonizers and now *mamoeiros* (papaya trees) grow very well in tropical climates of Brazil. Traditionally, papaya is eaten for breakfast with a squeeze of lime, blended into smoothies, cooked into a jam or candied into sweets. Green papaya is used raw in salads and on pages 48 and 68 you can discover more about the wonders of cooked papaya.

Manga—Mango
≈ mahn-gah

Mangoes are native to south Asia and were brought to Brazil by Portuguese colonizers. Mango trees—*mangueiras*—adapted extremely well to the warm climate and are now ubiquitous in Brazil. Throughout the book I call for ripe mangoes—the variety will vary depending on where you are, but seek out mangoes whose fragrance can be smelled through the skin and that are soft to the touch but not too mushy.

I also use mango juice in a few recipes. It's quite hard to find pure mango juice, so it's fine to use blends—my go-to is mango and apple juice, which is readily available. Avoid mango juices from concentrate or with added sugar or fake flavorings.

Manteiga de garrafa—Clarified butter/ghee
≈ man-tey-gah dje gah-ha-fah

Literally :bottle butter," so called because of its liquid state in the heat, *manteiga de garrafa* is clarified butter used particularly in north-east Brazil. The clarification process removes the milk solids and water which cause butter to spoil, so *manteiga de garrafa* can be stored at room temperature, making it practical in hotter climates. This process also imparts a rich, caramelized flavor.

I use clarified butter/ghee throughout the book—often in place of butter. This is because the clarification process removes most of the lactose, making it easier to digest and more nutritious.

To make your own, slowly heat butter to separate the milk solids and water from the fat, until the butter turns golden and smells slightly caramelized (you're *not* aiming for the dark brown of burnt butter). Strain the liquid and store in a clean jar.

Also known as: ghee in south Asian cuisine.
Where to buy: health food stores, some supermarkets.
Brands I like: Happy Butter, Fushi, Ghee Easy (always buy ghee in glass jars, avoid cans).
Substitution: melted butter.

Maxixe—West Indian gherkin
≈ mah-shee-shee

A small, spiky gourd native to West Africa that tastes sort of like a sour cucumber. Used in Afro-Brazilian cuisine in *maxixada* (a *maxixe* and salt beef stew) and also in fritters, soups, salads and pickles.

Also known as: West Indian gherkin in Caribbean cuisine.
Where to buy: Caribbean and African grocery stores.
Substitution: cucumber.

Pimenta—Chile
≈ pee-men-tah

Pimenta is the word for chile, but it can also refer to hot sauce (an abbreviation of *molho do pimenta*—literally "sauce of chile"). Brazil has an incredible array of fragrant chiles, including *malagueta, biquinho, cheiro, cão, chocolate* and *dedo de moça*. I tend to use Scotch bonnet and bird's-eye chiles when I'm cooking at home in London, because they're the most readily available hot and fragrant chiles. If you're in the US, fresh habanero is also a good option.

In Brazil, pretty much every restaurant and café will have hot sauce, whether store-bought or homemade. Just ask for "*molho de pimenta*," or simply "*pimenta*' as it's more commonly and casually referred to.

I *love* heat and use hot chiles liberally throughout the book. It goes without saying that you should always adjust chile amounts/types to your personal preference, adding a little bit at a time and tasting as you go to get your desired heat level.

Quiabo—Okra
≈ kee-ah-boo

Okra is native to West Africa and is predominantly cooked with in the states of Minas Gerais and Bahia. It's especially important in Afro-Brazilian cuisine, in dishes like *acarajé* and *vatapá*, which are rooted in the religious rituals of *Candomblé* (page 124).

Where to buy: Caribbean and African grocery stores, supermarkets.

Tapioca—Cassava starch
≈ *tah-pee-oh-kah*

Tapioca is a fine white flour made from cassava root starch. It's used as a binder or thickener, much like cornstarch in Western cuisine. It's traditionally used to make a sort of pancake (also called *tapioca*) which is usually filled with *manteiga de garrafa*, cheese, egg, ham, condensed milk, etc.

Also known as: tapioca flour or cassava flour in West African and Caribbean cuisine.
Where to buy: Brazilian, Caribbean and African grocery stores, some supermarkets, online.
Substitution: cornstarch.

Tucupi
≈ *too-koo-pee*

A sour yellow liquid extracted from toxic wild manioc, which is fermented and boiled before being used in Amazonian dishes like *pato no tucupi*, *tacacá* and *pimenta no tucupi* (page 194).

Substitution: see recipe on page 200.

Vinagrete
≈ *vee-nah-greh-chee*

Brazilian vinagrete resembles a textured salsa—a mix of finely chopped tomatoes, onions and cilantro, dressed with vinegar, oil and salt. It's served alongside grilled meats, fish or feijoada. You'll find several variations throughout the book (see pages 134, 143, 156, 170 and 202). Not to be confused with French "vinaigrette," which is a smooth, emulsified dressing.

Urucum—Annatto
≈ *oo-roo-koom*

Also known as *achiote* in Latin American cuisine and *annatto* in Caribbean cuisine, *urucum* (from the Tupi-Guarani language) is a shrub native to Central and South America. Its seeds are peppery, a little sour and have a vibrant orange-red hue. Indigenous people also use *urucum* for traditional body painting and cloth dyeing.

I buy a big bag of seeds online and grind them at home, but you can also find *urucum/annatto/achiote* as a paste or powder.

Also known as: *achiote* or *annatto* in Latin American and Caribbean cuisine.
Where to buy: Latin American, Carribean or Brazilian grocery stores, online.
Substitution: sumac + black pepper + sweet paprika.

Other things to note:

I always use sea salt—fine sea salt for cooking and sea salt flakes for finishing dishes. Himalayan salt is also great. Avoid iodized table salt if you can.

I cook with olive oil, coconut oil and ghee. I avoid refined oils like sunflower and vegetable oil, because they are bleached, deodorized and high in unhealthy trans fats. For deep-frying I use a mild-flavored olive oil and for shallow-frying I use a mix of olive oil and ghee.

I list liquids in grams because I find it easier just to measure ingredients straight into a bowl on a scale, but volume measures are included if that's your preference.

I avoid refined white sugar, usually opting for honey or maple syrup. They have more interesting, complex flavors and raise blood sugar less dramatically.

I cut my citrus into cheeks. This simply involves slicing off the flesh from the sides of the fruit, avoiding the central pith and seeds, giving you clean, juicy segments. You can then juice the central part, so nothing is wasted.

I use the green ends of scallions in many recipes. The white ends can be used to make stock or in any recipe that calls for finely chopped onions.

You can adapt my recipes to your dietary requirements and I've added in these handy symbols on each recipe:

GF—gluten-free
GFO—gluten-free option
V—vegetarian
VG—vegan
VGO—vegan option.

FLAVOR BOMBS

The concept of "Flavor Bombs" is something Yotam and I developed for *Ottolenghi Flavor*, and it continues to inform the way I cook. My fridge is always full of jars of marinades, pickles, oils and sauces that allow me to create meals full of flavor in minutes.

So I wanted to start the book with a carefully curated arsenal. These marinades, pickles, oils and sauces feature in recipes throughout *FUSÃO* but are also designed to ramp up the simplest of meals and to serve as building blocks to inspire your own creations.

People approach cookbooks in all kinds of ways. Some find comfort in following recipes to the letter and are happy to be guided towards great results. Others keep cookbooks on their bedside table and read them cover to cover, like novels. Some skim through methods, focusing on pictures and keywords, so they can riff off the recipe without following it too closely. Then there are those who just like to look at the beautiful pictures.

This book is for all of you. Of course I'd love you to cook your way through the book, find your favorite recipes and repeat them, but more than that, I hope that the recipes will spark ideas and encourage you to create combinations that feel uniquely yours.

The flavor bombs on the following pages serve two purposes. If you love sticking to recipes, I very much encourage you to spend a few hours stocking your fridge with these, so they're ready for you to use when they crop up in a recipe. For those who like to freestyle, they will serve as a foundation for you to come up with your own creations. Have fun using them in different ways, combining them and using them to add flavor, texture and color to your food.

Cashew coconut chile oil

Inspired by *salsa macha*, this chile oil uses cashews—*castanhas de cajú*—which are common in Brazil, and coconut oil for a healthier twist. Coconut oil sets at room temperature, so gently melt spoonfuls of the chile oil in a small pan on low heat when you want to use it. Alternatively, use MCT coconut oil if you can get hold of it, as it stays liquid at room temperature.

Makes 1 lb (500 g) — GF, V, VG
Prep time: 5 minutes
Cook time: 5 minutes
Cool time: 10+ minutes

- ⅓ oz (10 g) whole dried ancho or pasilla chiles
- ⅓ oz (10 g) whole dried cascabel chiles
- ⅛ oz (5 g) whole dried guajillo or pasilla chiles
- ⅛ oz (5 g) whole dried arbol chiles
- 1½ cups (350 g) coconut oil (preferably MCT coconut oil)
- ¾ oz (20 g) peeled garlic cloves (about 7), whole
- 1¾ oz (50 g) yellow onion (about ½ an onion), peeled and roughly chopped
- 1 cinnamon stick
- ⅓ oz (10 g) cilantro sprigs
- 2 tsp Aleppo pepper flakes
- 4 tsp (12 g) sea salt flakes
- ¼ cup (25 g) roasted and salted cashews
- 3 tbsp rice vinegar
- 1 tbsp maple syrup
- 1 tbsp (10 g) toasted black sesame seeds

Remove the stalks and seeds from the whole dried chiles.

Put the coconut oil, dried chiles, garlic, onion, cinnamon stick and cilantro sprigs into a large sauté pan and place on medium–high heat. Fry, stirring often, until the garlic becomes golden brown and the onion is lightly browned and translucent, about 5 minutes.

Remove the pan from the heat, add the Aleppo flakes and sea salt flakes and leave for 10 minutes.

Strain the oil through a sieve. Set the oil aside until cool and place the strained, fried ingredients on a separate plate.

Once the oil is completely cool, put it into a blender with all the strained, fried ingredients. Add the cashews, vinegar, maple syrup and sesame seeds and pulse until everything is very finely chopped—don't blend too much or you'll get a paste, you're after a textured oil with crunchy bits.

Divide between small jars and keep at room temperature for up to 2 months.

Ginger–garlic mix

This finely chopped mix of ginger and garlic forms the base of most of my meals—I always have a jar of this in my fridge. Use it as you would raw garlic—in stir-fries, marinades, sauces, salsas and stews. If you don't have the mix pre-made, use 1 small garlic clove and ⅛ oz (3 g) of peeled fresh ginger, very finely chopped, for each teaspoon of ginger–garlic mix. Add oil and salt to taste.

Makes 7 oz (200 g) — GF, V, VG
Prep time: 5 minutes

- 1¾ oz (50 g) fresh ginger, peeled and chopped
- 1¾ oz (50 g) peeled garlic cloves (about 17)
- ½ cup (100 g) olive oil
- 1 tbsp (9 g) sea salt flakes

Put the ginger, garlic, oil and sea salt flakes into a food processor and pulse until very finely chopped, scraping down the sides as needed. Transfer to a clean jar and refrigerate for up to 3 weeks.

Papaya or mango jam

You can make this jam with mango or papaya—both are equally delicious. Try either option on the corn cake (page 260) or the coconut rice pudding (page 244) instead of the guava-strawberry jam. They also work extremely well as a condiment to grilled/fried/roasted meat and fish, in which case I highly recommend adding 1 tablespoon of English mustard for a fiery kick.

Makes 12 oz (350 g) — GF, V, VGO
Prep time: 5 minutes
Cook time: 25 minutes

- 1 medium, extra-ripe papaya or 3 extra-ripe mangoes (about 1 lb 3 oz/1 kg)
- scant ½ cup (100 g) tangerine juice (3–4 tangerines)
- 3½ tbsp lime juice (2–3 small limes), plus ½ a lime to serve
- 3 tbsp honey (or maple/agave syrup)
- ⅓ oz (10 g) hunk of fresh ginger, roughly chopped
- 1 cinnamon stick
- 3 red bird's-eye chiles or 1 Scotch bonnet chile, whole
- 1 tsp rice vinegar
- 1 tsp vanilla bean paste

Peel the papaya or mango, remove the seeds/pit and chop the flesh into 1 in (3 cm) chunks. Put the chopped fruit into a 12 in (30 cm) wide pot and add all the other ingredients.

Place the pot on medium heat. Cook, stirring often, for about 25 minutes, until most of the liquid evaporates and the fruit softens. Use a spoon to mash the fruit and help break it down. Remove the ginger, cinnamon and chiles.

Finish with the juice of half a lime, transfer to a clean jam jar and refrigerate for up to 3 weeks.

Citrus pickled onions

I much prefer onions pickled in fresh citrus over vinegar, and here I use a mix of lime and tangerine to capture the flavor of my favorite *limão cravo* (page 21). These quick pickles are vibrant, zesty and add a pop of color to any savory dish.

Makes 13 oz (370 g) — GF, V, VG
Prep time: 10 minutes
Pickling time: 1 hour

- 2 red onions, peeled and halved lengthways
- ¼ cup (60 g) tangerine juice (2–3 tangerines)
- ¼ cup (60 g) lime juice (3–4 small limes)
- 1 tsp fine sea salt

Very thinly slice the onion halves into ⅛ in (4 mm) thick slices (with a mandoline if you have one).

Transfer to a large bowl with all the other ingredients and mix well so the onions are submerged in the liquid. Set aside for at least 1 hour for the color and flavor to develop, mixing every now and then.

Transfer to a clean glass jar and refrigerate for up to 2 weeks.

Tempero verde

Tempero means seasoning, but in this context it's closer to what we would call a sofrito. Brazilians use *temperos* as a finely chopped flavor base to start dishes with, or as a marinade. There are many versions of *tempero*—this one is made with herbs, garlic and ginger, but many also contain onions, bell peppers or chiles.

This *tempero verde*—green seasoning—is a fantastic marinade for meat, seafood and veg, but you can also use it as a fresh condiment for sandwiches, soups and stews, or in sauces and salsas.

Makes 8 oz (220 g) GF, V, VG
Prep time: 3 minutes

- ½ cup (100 g) olive oil
- 1¾ oz (50 g) scallions (around 3), roughly chopped
- 1 oz (25 g) cilantro
- 1 oz (25 g) fresh parsley
- ½ oz (15 g) garlic cloves (about 5)
- ⅓ oz (10 g) fresh ginger, peeled
- 1 mild green chile, stalk removed and roughly chopped
- 1 tsp fine sea salt

Put all the ingredients into a food processor and pulse to get a finely chopped paste, or very finely chop everything by hand.

Transfer to clean glass jars and keep refrigerated for up to 2 weeks.

Charred red pepper pimenta

This *pimenta*, a slightly thicker take on a hot sauce, makes a fantastic condiment or dipping sauce. It will firm up in the fridge, so gently warm it before serving to restore its silky texture.

Makes 10½ oz (300 g) GF, V, VG
Prep time: 3 minutes
Cook time: 12–17 minutes

- 4 red romano peppers
- 1 Scotch bonnet chile
- 2 large garlic cloves (¼ oz/8 g), peeled
- 2 tbsp olive oil
- ½ tsp fine sea salt
- 3 tbsp rice vinegar
- 20 twists of freshly cracked pepper (⅛ tsp)
- a little honey, to taste (optional)

Turn the oven to the highest broiler setting. Place the peppers and Scotch bonnet on a baking sheet and broil for 7–10 minutes, or until blackened in patches. Remove the Scotch bonnet, turn the peppers over and broil for another 5–7 minutes, until softened and blackened in patches on the other side.

Let the peppers and Scotch bonnet cool for a few minutes, then remove the seeds and stalks. Keep the blackened skin on, as it adds flavor. Place in a blender with the rest of the ingredients. Blend until completely smooth, then taste and adjust the seasoning—you may want to add a little more salt, vinegar or a bit of honey, depending on the size and sweetness of your peppers.

Transfer to a clean glass jar and keep refrigerated for up to 3 weeks.

Golden vinaigrette

This vinaigrette (not to be confused with "vinagrete," see page 23) pairs beautifully with steamed vegetables like leeks and asparagus. On page 105 I pair it with raw fish as an alternative to the grated tomatoes, and it also makes a fantastic condiment for oysters.

Makes 8 oz (220 g) — GF, V, VG
Prep time: 5 minutes
Cook time: 8 minutes

- 1 yellow/orange Scotch bonnet chile
- 4 oz (120 g) ripe orange/yellow tomatoes (about 2 medium)
- 3 tbsp olive oil
- 2 tbsp lime juice
- 2 tbsp rice vinegar
- 1½ tbsp (15 g) sea salt flakes

Put the Scotch bonnet into a dry frying pan on high heat and cook, turning, until well charred all over, about 8 minutes. Remove the stalk and seeds, then put the chile—along with its blackened skin—into a blender with all the remaining vinaigrette ingredients. Start with less chile and add more gradually, to taste, if you don't like too much heat.

Transfer to clean glass jars and keep refrigerated for up to 3 weeks.

Chopped red chile condiment

This chopped red chile mix is very hot, so wear gloves when handling the chiles if you're sensitive to chile burns.

If you're not a huge fan of heat, you can add less chile and/or you can temper the chile with drained, grated tomato. Add as much as you like to get your desired heat level.

Makes 12 oz (350 g) — GF, V, VG
Prep time: 5 minutes
Cook time: 5 minutes

- 3 Scotch bonnet chiles (1 oz/30 g)
- 10½ oz (300 g) mild red chiles, deseeded and roughly chopped
- 3 tbsp rice or apple cider vinegar
- 2 tbsp olive oil, plus extra to seal
- 1½ tbsp (15 g) sea salt flakes
- ⅓ oz (10 g) fresh ginger, peeled and roughly chopped
- ⅓ oz (10 g) garlic cloves (about 3), peeled and roughly chopped

Heat a frying pan on high heat, then add the Scotch bonnets and cook, turning, until charred all over, 4–5 minutes. Remove and discard the stalks and seeds.

Put the deseeded chopped red chile, the deseeded Scotch bonnet and all the remaining ingredients into a food processor and pulse until very finely chopped. Don't over-process— you want small pieces, not a paste.

Transfer to clean glass jars, cover with a thin layer of olive oil—just enough to cover the top—and refrigerate. Use within 3 weeks.

Pineapple pimenta

Make sure you're using very ripe pineapple for this hot sauce—that might mean leaving it to mature for a few days once you've bought it. You should be able to smell an intense pineapple flavor through the skin.

You'll use only half a pineapple here. You can use the other half for the pineapple torte (page 253) or double the recipe if you want to match a large batch.

I keep a bottle of this hot sauce in my fridge at all times. It goes incredibly well with grilled meat, seafood, on tacos or in any context you'd use hot sauce. It will keep in the fridge for up to 2 months and only gets better with time.

Makes 1 lb 5 oz (600 g) GF, V, VGO
Prep time: 5 minutes
Cook time: 10 minutes

- 3 Scotch bonnet chiles
- ½ a very ripe pineapple, peeled, core removed and chopped into 1½ in (4 cm) chunks (13 oz/380 g)
- 3 tbsp honey (or maple/agave syrup)
- ⅓ cup (80 g) rice vinegar
- 3½ tbsp lime juice (about 3 small limes)
- ¼ oz (8 g) fresh ginger, peeled
- 1 tsp fine sea salt
- ⅛ tsp ground cinnamon

Heat a frying pan on high heat. Once very hot, add the chiles and cook, turning every now and again, until nicely charred all over, about 8 minutes. Remove from the pan.

Add half the chopped pineapple to the pan and cook for 2 minutes, until charred on the bottom. Add the honey, swirling the pan as it liquifies, then immediately remove from the heat.

Once cooled a little, put the cooked pineapple and honey into a blender with the remaining fresh pineapple, vinegar, lime juice, ginger, sea salt and cinnamon. Blend until smooth.

Deseed the Scotch bonnets with a knife (or use gloves) and add in batches, blending and tasting as you go (don't remove the charred skin, this adds flavor). Depending on the heat of the chiles and your personal preference, you may or may not not want to add them all.

Strain the liquid through a sieve, squeezing the pulp to extract as much liquid as possible. Transfer the liquid to a clean jar or bottle and keep refrigerated for up to 1 month. Use the pulp in a salsa or as a condiment.

Chile-ginger tempero

This is lovely as a fresh condiment or stirred into salsas, and can also be used as a marinade or to add flavor to sauces, stews and soups.

Makes 8 oz (220 g) GF, V, VG
Prep time: 5 minutes

- 5¼ oz (150 g) red chiles, deseeded and chopped
- 1 oz (30 g) fresh ginger, peeled and roughly chopped
- ½ oz (15 g) garlic (4–5 cloves), peeled
- 1 tbsp rice vinegar
- ½ tbsp lime juice
- 1 tsp sugar
- ½ tsp fine sea salt
- Olive oil

Put all the ingredients into a food processor and pulse until very finely chopped. Transfer to a clean jar, cover with a layer of oil and keep refrigerated for up to 3 weeks.

Batata palha

Batata palha (literally, "potato straw") are fried potato sticks used as a textural topping. They're most typically scattered on top of *estrogonofe*—Brazil's version of stroganoff (page 206), but also on top of savory pies, lasagne, salads, etc.

You want smaller, gold potatoes for this. Avoid large potatoes as they are watery, and avoid pale or waxy potatoes.

Serves 4 as a topping	GF, V, VG
Prep time: 5 minutes	
Cook time: 6–18 minutes	

2 × 4½ oz (125 g) small gold potatoes, skin on and scrubbed clean
2¼ cups (450 g) light olive oil
sea salt flakes
freshly cracked pepper

Prepare a bowl of water and a tray lined with paper towels.

Slice the potatoes widthways with a mandoline to get ⅛ in (3 mm) thick slices. Cut into 1½ in (4 cm) long matchsticks, putting them into the water as you go. Swirl the potatoes in the water to remove the excess starch, rinse, then drain very well.

Spread the drained potatoes out on a clean, dry tea towel and dry thoroughly with paper towels.

Heat the olive oil in a medium pot on medium heat. Once the oil is very hot (350°F/180°C if you have a thermometer), fry the potatoes in batches so as not to overcrowd the pot. Scatter in some of the potatoes (take care as the oil may spit) and fry, stirring with a fork so they don't clump together, until crisp and golden brown, about 6 minutes.

Use a slotted spoon to remove the potato sticks from the oil, transfer to the lined tray and continue with the rest. Season with salt and pepper.

Yellow chile mash

This mash is extremely hot, despite the yellow peppers, which temper the fieriness of the yellow Scotch bonnets. Use sparingly; a small amount goes a long way.

Makes 10 oz (280 g)	GF, V, VG
Prep time: 3 minutes	
Cook time: 5 minutes	

2 yellow bell peppers (8 oz/240 g)
3½ oz (100 g) yellow Scotch bonnet or habanero chiles (or another hot yellow chile variety)
¼ cup (60 g) rice vinegar or apple cider vinegar
4 tsp (12 g) sea salt flakes

Turn the oven broiler to its highest setting.

Place the peppers and chiles on a rack set over a pan. Broil on the top rack of the oven for 5 minutes or until lightly blackened.

Leave to cool, then remove the stalks, seeds and pith from the peppers and chiles. Don't remove the blackened skin, this adds flavor.

Put into a food processor with the vinegar and salt and pulse until very finely chopped. Don't over-process—you want very small pieces, not a paste.

Transfer to clean jars and refrigerate. Use within 3 weeks.

Ingredients

VEGETABLES

Angu with roasted oyster mushroom & spiced tomato sauce

Angu (ang-goo), Brazil's version of polenta, is made with *fubá* (cornmeal) and water. Its name comes from *"agúm"* in the Fon dialect of West Africa and refers to yam porridge. With Portuguese colonization, corn was taken from central America to Africa and Brazil, transforming *angu* into the corn-based porridge it is today.

Angu is usually unseasoned, the logic being that it will balance out the sauce it's being served with. Not seasoning food is against my religion, so in this version I've flavored the *angu* with coconut milk, garlic, curry powder and Parmesan and I've turned it into a hearty, veg-based meal with the addition of roasted oyster mushrooms and a smoky tomato butter sauce.

Serves 4 — GF, V
Prep time: 5–10 minutes
Cook time: 36–37 minutes

1 lb (500 g) oyster mushrooms
3 tbsp olive oil
½ tsp fine sea salt
freshly cracked pepper

Spiced tomato sauce

4 tbsp olive oil
2 tbsp salted butter
4 garlic cloves, very finely chopped
1 mild red chile, deseeded and very finely chopped
½ tsp fine sea salt
5¼ oz (150 g) sweet, ripe cherry tomatoes, very finely chopped
1 tsp tomato paste
¾ tsp smoked paprika
⅛ tsp ground cinnamon
½ tsp chipotle or Urfa pepper flakes
freshly cracked pepper

Angu

1 × 14 oz (400 g) can of full-fat coconut milk
⅔ cup (150 g) water
⅔ cup (100 g) quick-cook polenta or fine cornmeal
3 oz (80 g) Parmesan (or vegetarian equivalent), finely grated
1 tbsp olive oil
1 small garlic clove, finely grated/crushed
½ tsp medium curry powder
½ tsp fine sea salt

To serve

⅛ oz (5 g) fresh chives, finely chopped
1 lime, halved

Preheat the oven to 410°F (210°C).

Line a large, baking sheet with parchment paper. Tear the mushrooms into halves, or quarters if they are large, and add to the baking sheet with the oil, salt and plenty of pepper and mix well. Spread out and roast for 20 minutes, then stir and roast for another 5 minutes, or until crisp and golden brown. Set aside.

Meanwhile, make the sauce. Put the oil and butter into a medium, nonstick frying pan and place on low heat. Once melted, add the garlic, chile and fine salt and very gently fry for 3–4 minutes, stirring often, until the garlic is soft and golden (you don't want the garlic to brown or become crispy, so keep the heat very low). Remove from the heat and immediately stir in the tomatoes, tomato paste, paprika, cinnamon, chile flakes and plenty of pepper. Set aside.

Put all the ingredients for the angu into a medium pot and whisk together. Place on medium heat and cook, whisking continuously, until completely smooth and thickened to a wet polenta consistency, about 6 minutes. If it starts to spit at any point, turn the heat all the way down.

Spoon the angu onto a platter, then spoon over the sauce, followed by the mushrooms. Drizzle over some more oil and finish with the chives. Serve with fresh lime.

Okra skewers with mango dressing

Quiabo (keeya-bo)—okra—is native to Africa and was brought to Brazil during the slave trade (see page 124). It's now ubiquitous in Brazilian cuisine and features in many classic dishes, most notably *frango com quiabo* (page 180).

I developed these skewers for my residency at The Standard Hotel in London in 2024. They turned out to be one of the most popular dishes, despite many guests' preconception that they didn't like okra. I adore the flavor and texture of okra, and what's more, it's extremely nutritious.

Serves 4 as a side — GF, V, VG
Prep time: 10 minutes
Cook time: 6 minutes

24 okra (10 oz/280 g)
2 bunches of scallions, green ends cut into 3 in (8 cm) lengths (use the whites in another recipe)
1 lime, halved

Mango dressing

⅓ cup (80 g) mango juice (see note)
2 tbsp olive oil
2 tbsp rice vinegar
2 tsp yellow chile mash (page 31) or ½ a Scotch bonnet chile, very finely chopped)
¼ tsp fine sea salt

Garlic yogurt

scant ½ cup (100 g) coconut or regular yogurt
1 small garlic clove, finely grated/crushed
¼ tsp toasted sesame oil
¼ tsp fine sea salt

Mix all the mango dressing ingredients together in a small bowl.

Mix all the yogurt ingredients together in a second small bowl.

Preheat the oven to 475°F (250°C).

Thread the okra and scallion pieces onto metal skewers. Arrange on a baking sheet. Brush each skewer with some of the mango dressing (stir it first to combine). If you don't have skewers, just place everything directly on the baking sheet.

Roast for 6 minutes near the top of the oven. The okra should be *just* cooked but still bright green and crunchy. Finish with a blowtorch, if you have one, until nicely charred.

Spread the yogurt on a platter and top with the skewers. Spoon over some more of the dressing and serve with fresh lime.

Note
Make sure you're using pure juice with no added sugar or fake flavorings. If you can't get pure mango juice, mango and apple juice would also work well, and pineapple juice would be a good alternative.

MINAS GERAIS

Minas Gerais (meaning General Mines) is an inland, highland state in the south-east of Brazil that borders the states of Goiás, Bahia, Espírito Santo, Rio de Janeiro, São Paulo and Mato Grosso do Sul. It's one of twenty-six states in Brazil and yet it's bigger than the whole of France, which goes some way to illustrate the vastness of Brazil.

What I love most about the region is the beautiful, verdant mountainscapes and the fact that there are *cachoeiras*—waterfalls—everywhere (I'm obsessed with waterfalls). Minas Gerais has 147 rivers running through it at various stages, hence its name *"a caixa d'água do Brasil»*—Brazil's water tank. This abundance of water is what makes Minas Gerais one of the most fertile states of Brazil, renowned for the production of corn, rice, beans, cassava, beef, cheese, coffee, cane sugar and *cachaça*.

Minas Gerais was extremely wealthy during its eighteenth-century heyday, following the discovery of gold, diamond, precious gem and iron ore mines, after which it is named. Due to its natural riches, it was one of the first areas to be settled by Portuguese colonizers, who enslaved or brutally killed the Indigenous people of the land. Minas Gerais is now famous for the colonial architecture of its UNESCO World Heritage towns, Ouro Preto, Tiradentes and Diamantina, which all boast impressive gilded Baroque churches nestled into the mountains.

The artistic riches and the architecture of the region are a reflection of the tireless work of millions of enslaved Africans forcibly taken to work in the mines. Indeed, many records show that more enslaved African people were taken to Minas Gerais than to all of the Americas. To this day, Minas Gerais is one of the most diverse areas of Brazil and this is reflected in the cuisine, which is a *fusão* of Portuguese, African and Indigenous influences.

Comida Mineira (Mineiran food) or "*comida da roça*"—a term describing nostalgic, home-cooked food from the countryside—is rich and hearty, made to feed miners and cattle ranchers. Typical ingredients are *fubá, quiabo, rapadura, queijo Minas, feijão, couve* and *ora-pro-nóbis* (cornmeal, okra, unrefined cane sugar, Minas cheese, beans, collard greens and ora-pro-nóbis).

Ora-pro-nóbis is the thick leaf of a thorny flowering shrub from the cactus family (pictured on page 43 in Heloísa's hands). It's extremely rich in antioxidants, vitamins and protein, so much so that it's also known as "*carne de pobre*," poor man's meat. It's pretty much exclusively cooked with in Minas Gerais (I haven't come across it in any other region), and it holds a lot of cultural significance. In the seventeenth century it used to be planted ornamentally around churches in the region. Enslaved people weren't allowed access to the plant but, aware of its nutritional and medicinal value, they devised a plan to harvest it. This was done during mass, after the priest said the words "*ora-pro-nóbis*" ("pray for us" in Latin), as this would be followed by a long prayer that served as a distraction.

Typically the leaves are cooked into stews with *costelinhas* or *frango* (pork ribs or chicken). Other classic *Mineira* dishes include *frango ao molho pardo* (a stew of chicken and its blood, page 190), *frango com quiabo* (chicken stew thickened with sliced okra, page 180), *angu* (thickened cornmeal porridge, page 35) and *bamba de couve* (pork and kale soup thickened with cornmeal or cassava). These dishes are traditionally made in *panelas de barro preto*—pots made from black clay and mangrove tree sap which are air-dried, then fired.

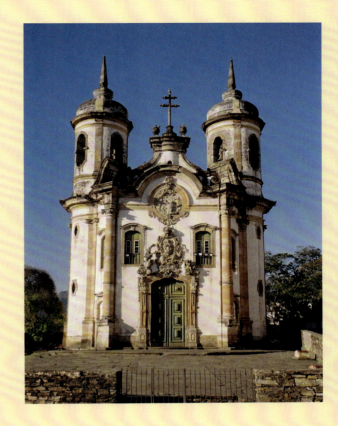

Vegetables

HELOÍSA

I first met Heloísa in 2023, after a treacherous drive through the mountains outside Ouro Preto. I'd come across Heloísa's *pousada* (BnB) during one of my obsessive Google maps deep dives (I'm addicted to spending hours zooming into the middle of nowhere in search of places off the beaten track). I stumbled upon Pousada Recanto do Salto, saw a picture of Heloísa cooking on a wood-burning stove and read a few reviews describing her warmth and hospitality. I instantly knew that we had to make the journey, that this was the perfect place to experience proper *comida Mineira—comida da roça*. I called ahead to book and set about planning the route, giddy with excitement at the prospect of everything I was going to eat.

What followed was a crazy journey. We took the long route up and over the *serra* (mountains) because I had my eye on a waterfall—*Cachoeira do Sibrão*—along the way. We drove up steep, rocky, iron-red dirt tracks in a car that was absolutely not built for the terrain. We encountered roads obstructed by fallen trees and with no signal for navigation, no road signs and countless forks in the road, we kept on having to gamble on which way to turn. Soon after, the fuel indicator started beeping incessantly, warning us that we were running dangerously low. It was boiling hot, we had no water, very little fuel and we were completely lost. To cut a very long story short, after driving directionless in the mountains for hours, we finally came across signs of life.

I have never been more grateful to arrive at a destination and I've never felt more welcomed. Heloísa received us like we were long-lost family. It feels hyperbolic to say this but it's true; her warm embrace felt like that of the grandmothers I'd never had.

We were parched, so she took my hand and led me into her *horta*—vegetable garden—to gather *folhas de cravo da Índia*—Indian clove leaves, which she blended with ice, *limão cravo* (a small lime with the flavor of tangerine, page 60) and *rapadura* (unrefined raw cane sugar) to make the most refreshing drink I've ever tasted. The clove leaves tasted like a combination of basil and clove—see page 274 for my take on this drink.

Once she was satisfied that her *limonada* had brought us back to life, she showed us around. We learned that her father had built the house from the ground up, that she had been born in the house—she showed us the very bed—and has lived there for seventy-seven years. I've been twice now and the magical feeling of being in a place steeped in so much history doesn't wear off.

Heloísa explained that her parents and grandparents were from this very area—Santo Antônio do Salto. I dug a little deeper and asked where her family were from before that. "*Turquia*"—Turkey—she responded, which got me incredibly excited, because of course the underlying message of this very book is that everything and everyone in Brazil is a bit of a *fusão*. I asked her if she ever cooked Turkish food and she responded with her cheeky smile and said, "*não, não há nada melhor do que a comida Mineira*"—"no, there is nothing better than Mineira food."

Heloísa's home is colorful and full of character: the kitchen shelves are lined with pots so shiny they might as well be mirrors, the ceiling is woven from wicker, and each of the adjoining bedrooms has breathtaking views of purple-flowered *ipê* trees, *bananeiras* and mountains in every shade of green.

In her *horta* she grows *quiabo, couve, ora-pro-nóbis, cebolinha, salsinha, coentro, gengibre, capim santo, cravo da Índia* (okra, collard greens, ora-pro-nóbis, scallions, parsley, cilantro, ginger, lemongrass, clove leaves). She has *bananeiras, mangueiras, palmeiras, mamoeiros* (banana trees, mango trees, palm trees, papaya trees).

She even has a small lake full of tilapia. Both times I visited she proudly asked, "*você sabe o que eles comem?*"—"do you know what they eat?" A rhetorical question as she ripped up *couve* leaves, tossed them into the lake and delighted as the fish jumped to gobble them up.

At the heart of her kitchen is a wood-burning stove. When we visited, it was covered in steaming, bubbling pots of classic *Mineira* dishes: *frango com quiabo, angu, costelinhas com ora-pro-nóbis* and *mamão refogado* (stir-fried papaya), to name a few.

I'd never eaten cooked papaya and I'll admit I was slightly wary, but as soon as I tried it I was hooked. It tasted sort of like mashed, roasted sweet pumpkin and I loved it so much I was inspired to create my own version, which you'll find on the next page. Heloísa makes her *mamão refogado* with green papaya as she doesn't like it too sweet. I love the combination of sweet and savory, however, so I've dialled into this, using sweet, ripe papaya in my version. I've also added fried scallions, curry powder and crispy basil and finished it with a squeeze of lime and a swirl of yogurt to temper the sweetness.

Stir-fried papaya with crispy basil

Cooked papaya tastes almost exactly like roasted pumpkin (I'd go as far as to say you wouldn't be able to tell the difference in a blind tasting). In this context, I've fried it with onion, green chile and curry powder and the result is like a sticky, sweet, roasted pumpkin mash (but made in a fraction of the time it would take to cook pumpkin). It tastes quite similar to a dish called *quibebé*, a spiced pumpkin or squash mash from north-eastern Brazil.

You need a ripe papaya for this—it should be soft and fragrant, with a dark orange interior.

Serve alongside meat or fish or as part of a veggie spread with rice or flatbreads.

Serves 6 as a side — GF, V, VG
Prep time: 10 minutes
Cook time: 17–19 minutes
(plus 2½ minutes if doing herbs)

- 1 large ripe papaya (3 lb/1.4 kg)
- 3 tbsp coconut oil
- 1 yellow onion, peeled and finely chopped (4 oz/110 g)
- 3 garlic cloves, peeled and roughly chopped
- 1–2 green chiles, thinly sliced
- ⅓ oz (10 g) scallion green ends, thinly sliced into rounds (use the whites in another recipe)
- ⅛ oz (5 g) fresh basil leaves, plus ⅓ oz (10 g) extra to make crispy basil (optional)
- ⅛ oz (5 g) cilantro leaves
- 1⅛ tsp fine sea salt
- 1 tsp medium curry powder, plus extra to serve
- 3 tbsp olive oil, plus ½ tsp for frying
- sea salt flakes
- 1 lime, halved
- ¼ cup (60 g) coconut or regular yogurt

Halve the papaya lengthways, scoop out the seeds, then scoop out the flesh and roughly chop it.

Put the coconut oil, onion, garlic, green chiles, scallions, ⅛ oz (5 g) of the basil, the cilantro and salt into a large sauté pan on medium heat. Stir-fry until the onion is soft and golden, about 7 minutes.

Add the papaya and the curry powder, then increase the heat to medium–high and continue to stir-fry for 10–12 minutes, until the papaya is soft and beginning to catch (this builds flavor). Stir in the olive oil and sprinkle with more curry powder and some sea salt flakes.

Squeeze over plenty of lime juice, stir in the yogurt and serve.

Optional
Top with crispy basil leaves. Preheat the oven to 475°F (240°C). Gently mix ⅓ oz (10 g) of basil leaves with ½ teaspoon of olive oil so that they are very lightly coated. Spread out on a baking sheet and bake for 2½ minutes, or until crisp but still bright green. You can also shallow fry in olive oil in a pan on the stove top. Serve on top of the stir-fried papaya.

Sweet potato gnocchi with spiced eggplant ragout

Making gnocchi from scratch can be a bit of a fuss, but this recipe keeps things simple. It serves two, since I rarely make gnocchi for a crowd, but you can easily scale it up.

In Brazil, *batata doce*—sweet potato—is the variety with the pink skin and yellow interior—in English it's sometimes known as "Japanese sweet potato" or "red sweet potato." This is the variety I grew up with and love; it's less sweet than the orange variety.

To bind the gnocchi and to keep them gluten-free, I've used masa harina, which is a type of nixtamalized corn flour used in Mexican cooking. It's not traditionally used in Brazilian cuisine, but it works really well here and keeps the gnocchi gluten-free.

Serves 2   GF, VO
Prep time: 15 minutes
Cook time: 1 hour 25 minutes

Gnocchi

1 lb (500 g) sweet potatoes (with pink skin and yellow interior)
1 egg yolk
½ cup (50 g) masa harina
½ tsp fine sea salt
plenty of freshly cracked pepper
plenty of freshly grated nutmeg

Ragout

2 medium eggplants (1 lb/500 g)
⅓ oz (10 g) fresh basil leaves, plus extra to serve
2 tbsp olive oil, plus extra for greasing
1 tbsp salted butter
1½ tbsp tomato paste
1 garlic clove, crushed
¾ tsp medium curry powder
¼ tsp fine sea salt
¼ tsp chile flakes
plenty of freshly cracked pepper
plenty of freshly grated nutmeg

To serve

grated Parmesan (or vegetarian equivalent)
zest of 1 lemon

Preheat the oven to 425°F (220°C). Line a baking sheet with parchment paper.

Leaving the skin on, cut the sweet potatoes into 6 oz (170 g) pieces (each about 5 in/12 cm). Halve the eggplants lengthways. Lightly brush the cut sides with oil and place them cut side down on the baking sheet with the potatoes.

Bake until the eggplants are soft and well browned on the bottom and the sweet potatoes are soft all the way through. This should take 45–50 minutes. Remove from the oven and cut slits in the potato pieces to help them cool.

While the potatoes are cooling, make the ragout. Scoop the eggplant flesh into a large frying pan off the heat (discard the skins). Add all the remaining ragout ingredients. Place on medium heat and cook for 4 minutes, stirring throughout. Set aside off the heat.

Scoop the sweet potato flesh into a bowl (discard the skin) and mash well to get rid of any lumps. You should have about 10½ oz (300 g) of mash. Add the egg yolk, masa harina, salt, pepper and nutmeg and mix very well.

Line a tray or large plate with parchment paper. Lightly grease the parchment paper with olive oil. Use 2 tablespoons to form pointed ovals of the gnocchi dough, placing them on the tray as you go.

Bring a pot of well-salted water to a boil. Once boiling, reduce the heat so the water is gently simmering. Add the gnocchi and cook until they all float to the top, about 4 minutes.

Use a slotted spoon to transfer the gnocchi to the ragout pot, along with a scant ½ cup (100 g) of the cooking water. Place the pot on medium heat and cook for a few minutes, gently stirring to combine the gnocchi with the sauce.

Finish with grated Parmesan, lemon zest, pepper, nutmeg, a drizzle of oil and more sea salt flakes if you like.

Note

Japanese or red sweet potatoes can be found in most grocery stores and Caribbean markets. Use regular orange sweet potatoes if you can't find them.

Roasted eggplant with mango sauce, lime yogurt & sesame salt

This is lovely alongside fish or meat, or as part of a vegetable spread with flatbreads and rice.

Serves 4 — GF, V, VG
Prep time: 10 minutes
Cook time: 40 minutes

- 3 eggplants, cut into 1 in (3 cm) thick rounds (1 lb 12 oz/800 g)
- 4 tbsp olive oil
- 2 tsp maple syrup
- 1 tsp ground urucum (aka annatto/achiote, see page 23), or use ½ tsp paprika + plenty of freshly cracked pepper
- 1 tsp fine sea salt
- ½ tsp chopped red chile condiment (page 29 or use fresh chopped chile)
- 2 scallions, green ends julienned (use the whites in another recipe)
- 2 limes, halved

Mango sauce

- 1½ cups (350 g) pineapple juice
- 1 cup (150 g) extra-ripe mango, finely chopped
- 3 tbsp freshly squeezed tangerine juice (from 2–3 tangerines)
- 1 yellow onion, peeled and cut into eighths
- 4 garlic cloves, peeled and crushed with the side of a knife
- 4 tbsp olive oil
- 4 allspice berries, roughly crushed
- 1 cinnamon stick, broken

Lime yogurt

- 1½ cups (350 g) coconut or regular yogurt
- 1 small garlic clove, finely grated/crushed
- 1 tsp lime zest
- ¼ tsp sea salt flakes

Sesame salt

- 2 tbsp sesame seeds
- ¾ tsp medium curry powder
- 1 tsp sea salt flakes (or more, to taste)

Preheat the oven to 475°F (250°C).

Put the eggplants into a large bowl with the oil, maple syrup, urucum, salt and chopped red chile condiment and mix well. Spread out on a large, flat, parchment paper-lined baking sheet.

Put all the mango sauce ingredients into a medium high-sided baking pan.

Place the eggplant pan on the top rack of the oven and the mango sauce pan on the bottom rack. Roast for 25 minutes, then flip the eggplants and roast for another 10 minutes, or until golden brown on both sides. At this point the onions in the mango sauce should be nicely browned around the edges and the sauce should have thickened a bit. Remove both pans from the oven and set aside to cool.

Combine all the lime yogurt ingredients in a medium bowl.

Toast the sesame seeds in a very hot pan until golden brown and fragrant. Put all the sesame salt ingredients into a mortar and roughly crush (not too much, you don't want a powder).

Plate as soon the eggplant and sauce have cooled a little (they should be just above room temp or they'll melt the yogurt). Spoon some of the lime yogurt onto a platter, then top with the roasted eggplants and some of the sauce (avoiding the allspice berries and cinnamon stick).

Finish with the green scallions and sesame salt and serve with fresh lime squeezed on top.

Coconutty saffron orzo with roasted squash

If you're looking for an impressive and beautiful vegan centerpiece that packs a punch, this is it. You can get ahead by pre-soaking and draining the orzo and pre-roasting the butternut.

To make this dish gluten-free, use 2 cups (400 g) of cooked rice instead of orzo—add it to the coconut milk sauce and cook until slightly thickened, about 7 minutes.

Serves 4   GFO, VGO
Prep time: 10 minutes
Cook time: 40 minutes

Orzo

9 oz (250 g) dried orzo pasta
1 × 14 oz (400 g) can of full-fat coconut milk
scant 1 cup (200 g) water
¾ tsp fine salt
½ tsp medium curry powder
½ tsp saffron threads
a generous pinch of grated or ground nutmeg
freshly cracked pepper

Roasted butternut

1 large butternut squash (2 lb 10 oz/1.2 kg), peeled, deseeded and chopped into ¾ in (2 cm) cubes (1 lb 12 oz/800 g)
1 regular red chile
1 Scotch bonnet chile (or a milder chile if you prefer)
3½ tbsp butter, cubed (or coconut oil to keep this vegan)
4 tbsp olive oil
2 tbsp white miso paste
2 tbsp maple syrup
2 tsp rose harissa
2 cinnamon sticks (or ⅛ tsp ground cinnamon)
½ tsp fine salt

To serve

⅛ oz (5 g) fresh parsley leaves
⅛ oz (5 g) fresh basil leaves
½ a small yellow onion, peeled and thinly sliced on a mandoline
2 tsp olive oil
⅛ tsp fine salt
1 lemon, halved

Preheat the oven to 475°F (240°C).

Put all the ingredients for the roasted butternut into a 12½ × 14 in (32 × 36 cm) high-sided roasting pan and mix well. Cover tightly with foil and bake for 15 minutes. Remove the foil and bake for another 25 minutes, stirring halfway, until soft and nicely browned.

Deseed and finely chop the cooked red chile and Scotch bonnet. Set aside.

While the butternut is roasting, put the orzo into a bowl and cover with freshly boiled water. Leave to soak for 10 minutes, then drain and rinse well under cold running water to separate the grains.

When the butternut is nearly ready, put the drained orzo into a 11 in (28 cm) sauté pan with the coconut milk, water, salt, curry powder, saffron and nutmeg. Mix well. Place on medium–low heat and cook for 14 minutes, stirring often, until the orzo is cooked through and the sauce has thickened—you're after the texture of a loose risotto. Stir in plenty of black pepper.

Spoon the orzo onto a platter and top with the roasted butternut. Toss the parsley, basil and onion together with the oil, fine salt and some or all of the chopped cooked chile, to taste. Arrange on top of the orzo. Squeeze over plenty of lemon juice and serve at once, as the orzo will set as it cools.

Corn & coconut pamonha in banana leaf with curried red pepper ragout

Pamonha (pa-mon-ya) is made from fresh corn which is grated or blended with coconut to make a paste, wrapped in corn leaves and then steamed. The word is derived from the *Tupi-Guarani* dialect word *"pa'muna,"* which means sticky, or *"apa-mimoia,"* meaning wrapped and cooked. Pamonha is traditionally eaten during the Festa Junina, a festival in the north-east which celebrates the end of the harvest and the beginning of winter.

Pamonha can be made sweet with condensed milk, cheese and guava jam, or savory, filled with meat and cheese. This untraditional version topped with a red pepper ragout happens to be vegan, making it a great option for an exciting veg centerpiece. I came up with it for my residency at The Standard Hotel, London, in 2024 and it went down a storm.

Makes 10   GF, V, VG
Prep time: 10–15 minutes
Cook time: 29–32 minutes

Ragout
1 lb 5 oz (600 g) red romano peppers
2 tbsp cashew coconut chile oil (page 26) or store-bought chile oil, plus extra to serve
1½ tbsp tomato paste
1 tbsp olive oil
1 tsp sea salt flakes
1 small garlic clove, grated or crushed
½ tsp medium curry powder

Pamonha
3 cups (500 g) frozen corn kernels, defrosted
¾ cup (120 g) quick-cook polenta or cornmeal
scant ½ cup (100 g) full-fat coconut milk (from a can, not a carton; mix well before measuring)
2 oz (60 g) yellow onion (about ½ an onion), peeled and roughly chopped
2 tbsp coconut oil, plus extra for greasing
1 tsp fine sea salt
½ tsp baking powder
½ tsp ground cumin
40 twists of freshly cracked pepper (about ¼ tsp)

Everything else
banana leaves, wiped clean on both sides
coconut or regular yogurt
scallion green ends, thinly sliced (use the whites in another recipe)
2 limes, halved

Start by making the cashew coconut chile oil, if using (page 26).

For the the ragout, turn the oven to the highest broiler setting. Place the peppers on a pan and broil for 7–10 minutes, or until soft and nicely charred in parts (but not completely burned). Turn the peppers over and grill until the other side is also soft and nicely charred in parts, about 7 minutes.

Cool, then deseed and remove some of the skin, leaving some on for color and flavor. Tear the peppers into strips and put them into a pan with the rest of the ragout ingredients. Place on medium heat and cook, stirring, for 5 minutes. Set aside.

For the pamonha, put all the ingredients into a food processor and blend until smooth, scraping down the sides as needed.

Preheat the oven to 450°F (230°C). Place a baking dish half-filled with water in the bottom of the oven to create steam.

Prepare a large, flat baking sheet. Cut ten rectangles (5½ × 6½ in 14 × 16.5 cm) out of banana leaves or parchment paper. Lightly brush with oil.

Spoon 3 oz (80 g) of the pamonha mix into the center of each banana leaf/paper. Use your hands to form into a 2½ × 3 in (6 x 8 cm) rectangle. Brush with a little oil. Fold the two longer sides of the banana leaf together to enclose the pamonha on either side (as per the photo overleaf). Place on the baking sheet, seam side up, while you continue with the rest. Once all the pamonha are formed, bake for 10 minutes, until just set, then set aside to cool for a few minutes.

Open the parcels and top with some of the ragout, followed by a spoonful of yogurt. Drizzle over some cashew chile oil and serve with sliced scallions and fresh lime squeezed on top.

Notes
Traditionally *pamonha* are wrapped in corn husks, but I love the look and flavor of banana leaves.

You can find banana leaves in some Asian supermarkets, often in the freezer aisle. Make sure you wipe the leaves clean on both sides once you've cut them into rectangles. Use parchment paper if you can't get hold of banana leaves.

CITRUS

My obsession with citrus is very much rooted in Brazil, where limes reign supreme and where *limão*—lime—is an umbrella term for many different varieties. The two main varieties are *limão galego*, which is smaller, seedy and intensely flavorful with high acidity, and *limão taiti*, which is larger, seedless and juicier.

Limão cravo (clove lime) is a small, round, orange-colored citrus fruit with the acidity of lime and the flavor of tangerine (but without the sweetness). It's extremely common, grows wildly in Brazilian backyards and is used to finish many dishes. Heloísa (see page 45) makes her *limonada* (page 274) with *limão cravo* and finishes her *frango com quiabo* (page 180) with its freshly squeezed juice. I adore this tangerine-y variety of lime, it's the best of both worlds. Indeed, the reason I often combine both tangerine and lime juice in my recipes is to recreate this flavor.

Lima da Pérsia (known *as* Palestinian sweet lime) is another variety that's very common in Brazil. It's small, round and green and has the flavor of tangerine, with slightly soapy, floral notes. Unlike *limão cravo,* it's sweet but not at all acidic. Because of this, it's a popular alternative to lime in *caipirinhas* for those who dislike acidity.

Lemons in Brazil are still relatively hard to come by and there is no single word in Brazilian Portuguese for lemon. Brazilians call lemons "*limão siciliano,*" which literally means Sicilian lime. For Brazilians, lemons aren't distinct from limes, they are simply a larger, yellow, less acidic variety. This all comes down to prevalence: limes are ubiquitous and grow pretty much everywhere in Brazil, whereas lemons—which fare well in Mediterranean and not tropical climates—are still seen as a luxury foreign ingredient. It's interesting to think about etymology with regard to prevalence in other languages, too. For example, in France, where limes don't grow, they are referred to as "*citron vert*"—"green lemon."

We all know the famous saying "when life gives you lemons, make lemonade," right? Well, in Brazilian Portuguese it's "*se a vida te der limões, faça uma limonada,*" which is understood as "if life gives you limes, make limeade." This really highlights the importance of limes in Brazilian culture.

Leeks with golden vinaigrette

There's nothing particularly Brazilian about this dish apart from the use of chile and leeks—*alho poró*—which are ubiquitous in Brazilian cuisine.

Inspired by the classic French dish but with a twist, the star of the show here is the yellow tomato and charred yellow Scotch bonnet vinaigrette, which would go really well alongside lots of other simply cooked veggies—asparagus, fennel, green beans, for example. It also works as a hot sauce, so make extra and bottle it up if you like.

Try to get yellow tomatoes that are almost orange or golden (avoid pale yellow ones) to make sure you get a really beautiful golden vinaigrette.

Serves 4 as a side	GF, V, VG
Prep time: 5–10 minutes	
Cook time: 24½–26½ minutes	

4 large leeks
1 cup (200 g) light olive oil
2½ tsp fine sea salt

Vinaigrette

1 yellow/orange Scotch bonnet chile
4 oz (120 g) ripe orange/yellow tomatoes (about 2 medium)
2 tbsp lime juice
2 tbsp rice vinegar
1¼ tsp sea salt flakes

Trim the tops of the leeks to leave them about 10 in (25 cm) long, keeping the roots intact. Reserve the green tops for frying.

Halve the leeks lengthways and arrange in the bottom of a 11 in (28 cm) pan, for which you have a lid. Make sure they're cut side up, but don't worry if you have to stack them on top of each other to get them to fit.

Sprinkle over the fine sea salt, then pour over a generous 2 cups (500 g) of water (this won't be enough to cover the top layer of leeks, but the steam created will be enough to cook all of them).

Place the pan on medium heat, cover with a lid and cook for 12–14 minutes, or until the leeks are soft but still bright green. Use tongs to gently transfer the leeks to a colander in the sink to drain, being careful to keep them intact.

Thinly slice/julienne 2 oz (60 g) of the reserved green leek ends into 2¾ in (7 cm) lengths (discard the rest of the green ends, or use for stock).

Put the sliced leek ends into a medium saucepan off the heat. Pour over enough oil to cover them (about 7 oz/200 g). Place on medium heat and fry, stirring throughout, until crisp but still green, about 4½ minutes. Remove the fried leeks with a slotted spoon and place on a plate lined with paper towels. Reserve 3 tablespoons of the frying oil.

Place the Scotch bonnet in a dry pan on high heat and cook, turning, until well charred all over, about 8 minutes. Remove the stalk and seeds, then put the chile—along with its blackened skin—into a blender with the rest of the vinaigrette ingredients (start with a small amount of chile and add more gradually to taste, if you don't like too much heat.) Add the 3 tablespoons of the reserved frying oil and blend until completely smooth.

Make sure the leeks are very well drained, then cut off the roots. Transfer them to a platter and sprinkle with sea salt flakes. If you have a blowtorch, lightly char the cut side of the leeks. Pour over some of the vinaigrette (you won't need it all) and finish with the crispy leek ends and some sea salt flakes.

See page 64 for a recipe photo. →

Tomato, mango & pickled onion salad

This refreshing salad is light, sweet and sour. You want a mango that's *just right*, not so ripe that it's soft and mushy, but not so unripe that it's rock hard. Cucumber would be a great addition for some extra crunch.

You'll need about 5 limes and 3 tangerines in total for this recipe.

Serves 4 as a side	GF, V, VGO
Prep time: 10–15 minutes	
Rest time: 2 hours	
Cook time: 2 minutes	

12 oz (350 g) ripe tomatoes, cut into bite-sized pieces and deseeded

6½ oz (180 g) yellow cherry tomatoes, halved lengthways

1½ tsp sea salt flakes

½ cup (100 g) light olive oil

¾ oz (20 g) small basil leaves

1 large mango, peeled and cut into bite-sized pieces

1 lime, halved

Pickled onions

1 red onion, halved lengthways and sliced ⅛ in (4 mm) thick on a mandoline

2 tbsp tangerine juice

2 tbsp lime juice

¼ tsp fine sea salt

Dressing

3 tbsp lime juice, plus extra to serve

2 tbsp tangerine juice

4 red bird's-eye chiles, thinly sliced into rounds (fewer if you prefer)

1 tbsp honey (or maple/agave syrup)

2 tsp rice vinegar

¼ tsp toasted sesame oil

¼ tsp fine sea salt

Put all the ingredients for the pickled onions into a small bowl and mix well. Set aside for at least 2 hours, for the color and flavor to develop.

Put the tomatoes into a large bowl and season generously with sea salt flakes.

Mix all the dressing ingredients together in a small bowl.

Put the oil into a medium saucepan on medium heat. Once hot, carefully scatter in the basil leaves—stepping back, as the oil may spit—and fry, stirring to separate the leaves, until bright green and crisp. Use a slotted spoon to transfer the crispy leaves to a plate lined with paper towels.

Drain the liquid from the tomatoes, then add the mango, drained pickled onions and dressing to the bowl and mix well.

Transfer to a platter and drizzle with some of the basil frying oil. Add more sea salt flakes to taste and a good squeeze of fresh lime. Finish with the crispy basil leaves and serve.

See page 64 for a recipe photo. →

Left Leeks with golden vinaigrette
Right Tomato, mango & pickled onion salad

Papaya & dendê dip

This is a great dip to serve with drinks (the guava caipirinha on page 274, for example) and is best scooped up with plantain chips and crunchy baby cucumbers.

To make your own plantain chips, start with hard, green plantains. Peel them, halve widthways, then use a mandoline to slice them into $\frac{1}{8}$ in (3 mm) thick slices. Fry in hot oil for about 4 minutes, until crisp, turning a few times, then transfer to a rack or tray lined with paper towels to soak up the oil. Salt generously while still warm.

Makes 1 lb 5 oz (600 g) — GF, V, VG
Prep time: 10 minutes
Cook time: 19 minutes

- 3½ oz (100 g) whole red chiles
- 1 oz (30 g) whole Scotch bonnet chiles
- ½ cup (100 g) mild olive oil
- 1¾ oz (50 g) yellow onion (about ½ an onion), peeled and roughly chopped
- 1 oz (30 g) garlic cloves (about 10), peeled and roughly chopped
- ⅓ oz (10 g) fresh ginger, peeled and roughly chopped
- ⅛ oz (5 g) dried cascabel or pasilla chiles, stalks and seeds removed
- ½ cinnamon stick, broken up
- 1 tsp mixed peppercorns
- ½ extra ripe papaya, peeled, deseeded and finely chopped into ¼ in (¾ cm) cubes (10½ oz/300 g)
- heaped 2 tbsp tomato paste
- 2 tbsp red palm oil (see page 20)
- 2 tbsp rice vinegar
- 1 tsp fine sea salt
- 2 tbsp lemon juice
- 2 tsp maple syrup
- 1 lime, to serve

Heat a frying pan on high heat. Once hot, add the whole red chiles and Scotch bonnets and cook until nicely charred on both sides (about 4 minutes each side).

Remove the stalks, seeds and pith from the chiles and roughly chop them. Let the pan cool down completely.

Return the deseeded chiles to the cooled pan with the oil, onion, garlic, ginger, cascabel, cinnamon and peppercorns. Place on medium heat and cook, stirring often, until the onions and garlic are soft and a light golden brown, about 6 minutes. Make sure they don't burn or get crispy.

Strain the oil through a heatproof sieve set over a heatproof bowl. Transfer the strained solids to a chopping board, discard the cinnamon stick, then chop everything very finely (use a food processor if you prefer).

Put the chopped mixture and the strained aromatic oil back into the pan. Add the papaya, tomato paste, palm oil, vinegar and salt, gently mix and cook over a low heat for 5 minutes, stirring often.

Remove from the heat and finish with the lemon juice and maple syrup. Serve slightly warm or at room temperature, as the oil will set if cool.

Serve with chips, cucumbers and plenty of fresh lime squeezed on top.

Ginger-garlic-cilantro fries

I really hate deep-frying, so whenever I feel like fries I always opt for oven-baked. They might not be quite as crisp but they are so much tastier, in my opinion, especially with the addition of ginger, garlic, cilantro and lime. The best potatoes for fries are starchy varieties like Russet. Avoid pale, watery and waxy potatoes.

Serves 4 as a side	GF, V, VG
Prep time: 5–10 minutes	
Cook time: 35 minutes	

1 lb 3 oz (1 kg) roasting potatoes, skin on and scrubbed clean
2 tbsp olive oil
1 tsp fine sea salt
freshly cracked pepper
2 tbsp ginger–garlic mix (page 26)
¾ oz (20 g) picked cilantro leaves
sea salt flakes
1 lime, halved

Preheat the oven to 425°F (220°C).

Line the largest baking sheet that will fit into your oven with parchment paper.

Leaving the skin on, cut the potatoes into fries approximately ½ in (1 cm) thick and 2¾ in (7 cm) long.

Toss the fries with the oil, salt and plenty of pepper and spread them out as much as possible on the pan (see note). Bake for 25 minutes on the middle rack of the oven.

Remove from the oven and add the ginger–garlic mix and the cilantro, then use the parchment paper to help you mix everything together. Be very gentle, as the fries will still be quite soft.

Return them to the oven and bake for another 10 minutes. Toss the fries a couple of times so they color evenly and keep an eye on them throughout, taking them out when they're at your ideal level of golden brown and crisp. Sprinkle with sea salt flakes, squeeze over some lime and serve.

See page 135 for a recipe photo. →

Note
Use a large baking sheet and avoid overcrowding it, as the potatoes need space and surface area to color and crisp up. If your tray isn't large enough, use two, in which case the cook time may be a little longer.

Stir-fried watercress with garlic & chile

Watercress—*agrião*—is widely used in Brazilian cuisine: most famously in the classic stew *rabada com agrião* (oxtail with watercress), but also in many other stews and soups, or simply fried on its own. I'm completely obsessed with watercress and tend to have a few bunches in my fridge at all times to quickly add to soups and stews. If you're looking for a simple green side dish, look no further than stir-fried watercress, which is ready in a matter of minutes, rich in antioxidants and, most importantly, extremely tasty.

Use the ginger–garlic mix (page 26) instead of the sliced garlic if you have some already made.

Serves 2 as a side — GF, V, VG
Prep time: 3 minutes
Cook time: 4–5½ minutes

- 3 tbsp olive oil
- 2 garlic cloves, very finely sliced
- 3 red bird's-eye chiles, thinly sliced into rounds (use less or a milder chile if you prefer)
- ½ tsp sea salt flakes
- 8 oz (240 g) watercress
- juice of ½ a lemon or lime

Put the oil, garlic, chiles and sea salt flakes into a large sauté pan or wok on medium–low heat. Gently stir-fry until the garlic is soft and golden—2–3 minutes—taking care not to burn it.

Add the watercress to the pan, increase the heat to medium-high and stir often to make sure you don't burn the garlic or watercress. Cook until the watercress is wilted but still bright green, 2–2½ minutes.

Remove from the heat, squeeze over the lemon or lime juice, stir and serve immediately.

See page 72 for a recipe photo. →

Note
I use a 12½ in (32 cm) pan. If yours is smaller, add the watercress in stages, letting the previous batch wilt a little before adding more.

Top Stir-fried watercress with garlic & chile
Bottom Couve & blood orange salad

Couve & blood orange salad

Traditionally *feijoada* (pork and black bean stew) is served with sautéed *couve* (a type of cabbage similar to collard greens or young cabbage) as well as orange slices. The combination of orange slices with black beans always causes a lot of confusion for those who have never tried it, but trust me when I tell you Brazilians know what they're doing—the sweetness and acidity of the orange perfectly cuts the richness of the beans.

This is an appropriately zingy accompaniment to the *feijão* on page 88. It's a happy mix of cabbage and orange but in salad form, with some herbs and sugar snaps thrown in for texture.

Serves 4 — GF, V, VGO
Prep time: 10–15 minutes

Dressing

- juice of 1 lemon
- juice of 1 lime, plus ½ a lime to serve
- ⅓ oz (10 g) fresh ginger, peeled and finely grated
- 1¼ tsp sea salt flakes
- 2 tbsp olive oil, plus extra to serve
- 1 tbsp honey (or maple/agave syrup)
- 1 tsp rice vinegar
- ½ tsp Aleppo pepper flakes/pul biber (or regular chile flakes), plus extra to serve

Salad

- 3 blood (or regular) oranges
- 3½ oz (100 g) young cabbage, collard greens or green cabbage, thinly sliced
- 5¼ oz (150 g) sugar snap peas, halved diagonally
- ¾ oz (20 g) scallions, green ends thinly sliced into rounds (use the whites in another recipe)
- ⅛ oz (5 g) fresh basil
- ⅛ oz (5 g) fresh mint
- 1 green chile, thinly sliced into rounds

Put all the dressing ingredients into a large bowl and whisk together.

Use a sharp knife to peel the oranges, then slice them into rounds. Add half the orange slices (along with their juice) to the bowl of dressing.

Just before serving, add the cabbage, sugar snaps, scallions, herbs and green chile to the bowl. Gently toss, then transfer to a platter.

Finish with the remaining orange slices, a drizzle of oil and a sprinkle of chile flakes. Squeeze over some lime juice and serve.

Coconut & ginger roasted cherry tomatoes

These tomatoes couldn't be simpler and are the perfect condiment to serve with seafood or meat. They're also great on toast, with eggs, in sandwiches or baked potatoes, with rice or noodles. Essentially they go with absolutely everything savory.

These will keep for up to a week in the fridge (and their flavor will improve with time), but they're are best served slightly warm, as the coconut milk will set when chilled.

To make this a meal, add fish fillets to the baking dish after 25 minutes, spoon over some of the tomatoes and sauce and return to the oven for 10 minutes. You can also do this with peeled raw shrimp, in which case they'll need only a few minutes in the oven.

Serves 4 GF, V, VGO
Prep time: 5 minutes
Cook time: 35 minutes

Tomatoes

1 lb 3 oz (1 kg) ripe, sweet cherry tomatoes (such as Datterini)

scant 1 cup (200 g) full-fat coconut milk (from a can, not a carton; mix well before measuring)

1 oz (30 g) fresh ginger, peeled and cut into short, thin matchsticks

1 oz (30 g) cilantro

6 whole bird's-eye chiles (a mix of green and red)

6 garlic cloves, peeled and left whole

2 tbsp honey (or maple/agave syrup)

1 tsp ground turmeric

1 tsp fine salt

To serve

olive oil

1 lime, halved

Preheat the oven to 475°F (250°C), or as high as your oven will go.

Put all the ingredients for the tomatoes into a baking dish that's just big enough to fit everything snugly in a single layer (a 15 in/38 cm oval dish is perfect for this). Mix well, then roast for 35 minutes, or until the tomatoes are charred and the sauce is bubbling.

Drizzle with a little oil and serve warm, with fresh lime squeezed on top. Chop the chiles and stir them back into the sauce if you want more heat.

Charred sweet & sour peppers

There are so many ways to use these charred red peppers—as an antipasto, on crostini, in sandwiches, mixed into salads or served alongside grilled meat or seafood. They also pair really well with raw fish, especially tuna.

Serves 4 — GF, V, VG

Prep time: 5–10 minutes
Marinade time: 1 hour
Cook time: 10–17 minutes

6 red romano peppers
1 Scotch bonnet chile

Marinade

scant ½ cup (100 g) tamari or soy sauce
½ oz (15 g) fresh ginger, peeled and julienned
2 garlic cloves, crushed with the side of a knife
⅛ oz (5 g) cilantro sprigs
⅛ oz (5 g) fresh basil sprigs
1 tbsp rice vinegar
1 tbsp lime juice
1 tbsp tangerine juice
1 tbsp olive oil
1 tsp maple syrup
⅛ tsp fine sea salt

Turn the oven to the highest broiler setting. Place the peppers and Scotch bonnet on a pan and broil for 7–10 minutes, or until soft and blackened in parts. Remove the Scotch bonnet, then turn the peppers over and broil for another 3–7 minutes, or until the other side is also soft and blackened in parts.

Put all the marinade ingredients into a container.

Remove the seeds and stalks from the peppers and Scotch bonnet.

Rip the peppers into strips—I like to keep most of the charred skin, but you can remove it if you prefer.

Add the pepper strips to the marinade. Finely chop the Scotch bonnet and add it bit by bit, stirring and tasting as you go, to get your desired heat level (I tend to add it all).

Leave to marinate for at least 1 hour before serving.

Sweet & sour carrots with hot sauce & lime

These roasted carrots are super simple and make the perfect accompaniment to fish and meat.

Serves 4 — GF, V
Prep time: 10–15 minutes
Cook time: 30–35 minutes

Carrots

- 1 lb 3 oz (1 kg) carrots, peeled and cut at an angle (see photo opposite)
- 3½ tbsp softened ghee or salted butter, in small pieces
- 3 tbsp honey (or maple/agave syrup)
- ½ oz (15 g) fresh ginger, peeled and julienned
- 3 garlic cloves, finely chopped
- 2 tbsp olive oil
- 1½ tsp Aleppo pepper flakes/pul biber
- a good grating of nutmeg
- ½ tsp fine sea salt
- plenty of freshly cracked pepper

To finish

- 1 tbsp hot sauce (preferably the pineapple pimenta on page 30, or use a store-bought hot sauce)
- 1 lime, halved
- sea salt flakes

Preheat the oven to 425°F (220°C).

Line a large baking sheet with parchment paper.

Put all the carrot ingredients into a bowl and mix very well. Tip onto the lined baking sheet and spread out.

Roast for 15 minutes, then mix well and roast for another 15–20 minutes, or until the carrots are sticky, golden brown and caramelized.

Add the hot sauce, then squeeze over the lime juice. Finish with some sea salt flakes, mix well and serve.

Blood oranges with chile ginger–garlic oil

No *feijoada* (see page 20) is complete without sliced oranges. Those who didn't grow up eating black beans with oranges will likely find the combination odd, but any Brazilian knows that the sweetness and acidity of the orange is the perfect counterpart to the fatty, salty pork and beans—this recipe was created with this in mind.

This salad features a chile ginger–garlic oil, lime, lemon, ginger, pickled onions and green chiles. It might sound like there's a lot going on, but it goes incredibly well with the chocolate-spiked *feijão* and the guava, curry & chile meatballs on pages 88 and 226. It would also be lovely with raw tuna or another fish as a crudo, or alongside roast pork or chicken.

Serves 4 as a side	GF, V, VG
Prep time: 10 minutes	
Cook time: 3½ minutes	

Chile ginger–garlic oil

- 2 tbsp ginger–garlic mix (page 26)
- 2 tbsp olive oil
- 1 tsp Aleppo pepper flakes/pul biber (or ½ tsp regular chile flakes)
- 1 tsp Urfa pepper flakes (or ¼ tsp chipotle chile flakes)

Everything else

- 1 small red onion, peeled and halved lengthways
- 1 lemon, halved
- sea salt flakes
- 4 blood oranges
- ¾ oz (20 g) fresh ginger, peeled
- 1 lime, halved
- 1 tsp maple syrup
- 1 green chile, thinly sliced into rounds

Put the ginger–garlic mix, 1 tablespoon of the olive oil, the Aleppo pepper and Urfa pepper into a small saucepan. Place on low heat and very gently fry, stirring, for about 3½ minutes, or until the garlic is soft and golden. Make sure you keep the heat low—you don't want crispy or burned garlic. Remove from the heat and add the remaining tablespoon of oil.

Thinly slice the onion (with a mandoline if you have one), then put it into a bowl with the juice of the lemon and ½ tsp sea salt flakes. Mix well.

Slice the blood oranges. Remove the skin and pith with a sharp knife, then slice widthways into ¼ in (¾ cm) thick rounds. Arrange on a platter and sprinkle over ½ teaspoon of sea salt flakes.

Finely grate the ginger (with a microplane, if you have one), then squeeze the ginger pulp through a sieve over a small bowl to get about 2 teaspoons of ginger juice. Add the juice of a lime and the maple syrup and mix. Spoon evenly over the oranges.

Drizzle over some of the chile ginger–garlic oil and finish with the pickled onions and green chile.

Chilled avocado soup with scallion butter

In Brazil, avocado is usually eaten in a sweet, rather than a savory context—in ice cream, as a snack with honey or in smoothies called *abacatadas*, which are made with milk, sugar and lime juice (or sometimes with condensed milk).

I often talk to my mom about her memories of the kitchen at her grandparents' house; what they used to cook, what their favorite dishes were. One of my great-grandfather's favorite traditions was to end each meal with an *abacatada* and it's something I think about a lot.

Personally, I prefer avocado in a savory context, but nevertheless this soup is a nod to my great-grandfather—a sort of *abacatada salgada* (savory *abacatada*), which I hope he would appreciate.

Serves 4 — GF, V
Prep time: 5–8 minutes
Cook time: 5–6 minutes

Soup

- 2 ripe avocados, peeled and pitted (9½ oz/270 g)
- 1¼ cups (300 g) coconut milk (from a carton, not a can)
- scant ½ cup (100 g) water
- zest and juice of 2 limes
- 2 tbsp olive oil
- 1¾ oz (50 g) spinach leaves
- 1 green bird's-eye chile (less/more if you prefer)
- ⅓ oz (10 g) scallion green ends (use the whites in another recipe)
- ⅓ oz (10 g) fresh mint leaves
- ⅓ oz (10 g) fresh basil
- ⅛ oz (5 g) cilantro
- ⅛ oz (5 g) fresh ginger, peeled
- 1½ tsp fine sea salt

Scallion butter

- 4 tbsp (60 g) salted butter
- 2 tbsp olive oil
- ¾ oz (20 g) scallion green ends, thinly sliced into rounds (use the whites in another recipe)
- 2 small garlic cloves, finely chopped
- 1 green bird's-eye chile, thinly sliced into rounds

To serve

- coconut or regular yogurt, or sour cream
- lime

Put all the ingredients for the soup into a blender and blend until completely smooth. The texture should be pourable; add more liquid if needed. Chill while you make the butter.

For the butter, put all the ingredients into a medium pot on medium–low heat and gently cook for 5–6 minutes, or until the butter has melted and the garlic is starting to become a little crisp. You don't want to brown the garlic, so take care not to overcook it.

Pour the soup into bowls and finish with a spoonful of yogurt or sour cream, a spoonful of the garlic butter, some lime zest and lime juice.

MUSIC, POLITICS, FOOD

I've noted a few times that this book barely scratches the surface of Brazil, that Brazil defies being fully captured, and this book doesn't try to. As such, there are countless topics I don't cover, but it would be remiss of me not to mention two very important subjects—music and politics—and touch upon how they are inextricably intertwined and how they relate to my family (and the fact that I'm sitting here, writing this).

Growing up, I was surrounded by the music of Brazilian greats. The sounds of Maria Bethânia, Chico Buarque, Jorge Ben Jor, Gal Costa, Rita Lee, Caetano Veloso and Gilberto Gil blasted from the speakers, my mother unabashedly and joyfully singing along at the top of her lungs, as is the Brazilian way. My mom has a tradition of having "*feijoada* parties," where she invites a crowd of Brazilians to eat together but, more importantly, to sing together. When Brazilians come together to sing, the air is electrically charged with raw emotion—it's something that has to be witnessed to be understood—and these parties are some of my most treasured memories.

Brazil is known around the world for its music. On the surface most songs sound joyful and uplifting, and indeed many are, but more often than not, the lyrics have deeper meanings and are a vehicle for delivering powerful cultural and political messages.

The origins of samba tell this story clearly: born from the resilience of enslaved Africans who endured unimaginable hardship, samba arose as a rhythm of survival and defiance, blending sounds from Africa with Indigenous and European influences. Samba is in itself a *fusão*. What began as a quiet expression of resistance grew into the defining sound of Brazil. Today, samba pulses through Carnaval and beyond, celebrating a legacy of resilience.

In 1964, Brazil's military overthrew President João Goulart, leading to a right-wing dictatorship regime marked by censorship and human rights abuses. My mother's father was a left-wing activist involved in a pilots' trade union in the north-east of Brazil, and as such, was forced into exile. To cut an extremely long story short, because of this, my mother, her siblings and my grandparents left Brazil for a while, headed for Cuba, via Mexico. In Cuernavaca, Mexico, they stayed in a halfway house for left-wing political refugees, which just so happened to be run by my father's father, who had himself been deported from America for his ties to communism. This was where my parents first met and from the garden of my grandfather's house in Cuernavaca you can see the volcano Ixtaccíhuatl (from the Nahuatl language), after which I'm named.

Cut back to Brazil under the military dictatorship, a horrific time in Brazilian history during which around 500 people were killed, 20,000 tortured and tens of thousands exiled. During this period, everything was censored, including music. Music has always been political in Brazil, but throughout that time musicians weren't allowed to allude to anything that might paint a negative picture of colonialism, slavery, the military regime and anything in between. They had to get clever about it: I'll give you an example.

Chico Buarque was (and is) a lyrical genius who used his music to subtly challenge Brazil's military dictatorship. He crafted songs with double meanings that resonated both as popular anthems and as veiled critiques of the oppressive regime. "Vai Passar" is one such masterpiece. On the surface, it's a joyful, upbeat anthem of Carnaval, a time when people from all walks of life come together to celebrate. When you delve into the lyrics, however, you uncover a layered message. Through lyrical mastery, Chico reflects on Brazil's colonial past and the horrific legacy of slavery, while also hinting at the injustices of the dictatorship. Please go and listen to "Vai Passar" and read a translation of the lyrics as you do! Despite joyful overtones, an important political message lies beneath.

How does politics and music link to food? Well, first of all, food IS political and anyone who says otherwise is delusional. Again, I'd need a whole book to cover this topic and there are not enough pages here, so I'll leave you with some examples of songs about food, of which there are countless in Brazil. Please go and listen to them while you cook!

"Feijoada Completa"—Chico Buarque
"Tropicana (Morena Tropicana)"—Alceu Valença
"Tico-Tico (No Fubá)"—Carmen Miranda
"Vatapá"—Dorival Caymmi
"Açai"– Djavan
"Bananeira"—João Donato and Gilberto Gil
"Bis"—Arthur Verocai

Feijão with chocolate & spices

Purists may dislike the inclusion of seaweed, ginger, Worcestershire sauce, curry powder and chocolate here, but then this is not the recipe for them.

Soaking the beans overnight not only softens them so they cook quicker, it also makes them *much* easier to digest. Years of testing and tasting has left me with a sluggish digestive system, so for me, this is especially important.

My mom has always made *feijão* with ginger, seaweed and cumin for two reasons: flavor primarily, but also because these three ingredients in conjunction help to stimulate digestive enzymes and reduce inflammation in the gut. So although this may not be the traditional way of making beans, it's nostalgic for me.

The addition of chocolate lends a rich, lightly sweet depth. It's completely untraditional and optional, but highly recommended.

Serves 6 — GF, VO
Prep time: 5 minutes
Soak time: overnight
Cook time: 2 hours 5 minutes

- 2⅔ cups (500 g) dried black turtle beans
- ⅛ oz (5 g) kombu or another dried seaweed
- 2 oz (60 g) diced pancetta or bacon lardons (optional)
- 1 Scotch bonnet chile or a milder chile if you prefer (optional)
- 3 oz (80 g) dark chocolate, broken into pieces

Umami paste

- 3 oz (80 g) yellow onion (1 small onion), peeled and roughly chopped
- 3½ tbsp tomato paste
- 3½ tbsp olive oil
- ½ oz (15 g) garlic cloves (about 4), peeled
- ⅓ oz (10 g) fresh ginger, peeled
- 2 tbsp Worcestershire sauce, plus extra to finish
- 1 tbsp rice vinegar (or another vinegar)
- 2 tsp fine sea salt
- 1¼ tsp ground cumin
- ¾ tsp medium curry powder
- ⅛ tsp sweet paprika
- ⅛ tsp chile powder
- 30 twists of freshly cracked pepper (⅛ tsp)

Soak the beans overnight, making sure they are very well covered with water as they'll expand *a lot*. Drain the beans the next day.

Put all the paste ingredients into a food processor and blend until smooth. Put the paste into a 11 in (28 cm) Dutch oven or heavy-bottomed pot, for which you have a lid, then add the drained beans and seaweed, with the pancetta and Scotch bonnet (if using).

Cover with 5 cups (1.15 liters) of water, stir and cover with the lid. Place on low heat and cook for 1 hour and 45 minutes, or until the beans are soft all the way through; lift the lid every now and then and stir the beans so they cook evenly. Taste and remove the Scotch bonnet at any point if you feel the beans are becoming too spicy.

Once the beans are soft, remove the lid. Increase the heat to medium and cook, stirring often, until the liquid reduces and thickens to the consistency in the picture (this could take up to 20 minutes).

Remove from the heat and stir in the chocolate. Check the seasoning—I tend to add another 1¼ teaspoons of fine sea salt (see note) and a few more splashes of Worcestershire sauce at this point.

Note
Beans need *a lot* of salt. You may feel the amount I've included is excessive, which is why I've added it in stages; you can stop adding whenever you like, but I predict you'll need it all.

Roasted root vegetables with maple, lime & chile

This is great alongside steak, roast chicken or fish. I love the variety and color of all the different veggies here, which end up looking as beautiful as a painting.

Serves 4 as a side — GF, V
Prep time: 5 minutes
Cook time: 1 hour 23 minutes

Veg

2 medium purple sweet potatoes
2 medium orange sweet potatoes
3 medium beets, with about 2 in (5 cm) of stalk left on
1 large red onion
olive oil
fine sea salt

Everything else

6 tbsp (80 g) butter, chopped into pieces (or a dairy-free alternative)
sea salt flakes
juice of 2 limes
2 tbsp maple syrup
1 tbsp Worcestershire sauce
1 whole nutmeg
1 whole dried habanero (or a pinch of chile flakes)
a good pinch of garam masala
coconut or regular yogurt or sour cream (optional)

Preheat the oven to 425°F (220°C).

Scrub all the veg clean, keeping them whole and skin-on. Poke holes all over them with a fork, then put them into a 10 × 14 in (25 cm × 35 cm) high-sided roasting pan.

Add 2 tablespoons of oil and ½ teaspoon of fine sea salt and mix well so the vegetables are evenly coated.

Pour in a scant ½ cup (100 g) of water, then cover tightly with foil. Bake for 1 hour and 15 minutes, or a bit longer depending on the size of your roots—everything should be soft all the way through.

Remove the pan from the oven and carefully pour any roasting juices into a bowl.

Turn the oven to the highest broiler setting.

Once cool enough to handle, use the tip of a sharp knife to slice the sweet potatoes and onion open (don't cut all the way to each end), then squeeze the ends in to push the flesh up and out.

Quarter the beets (or halve them if they're small).

Stuff the butter into the sweet potatoes and onion. Drizzle oil evenly over all the veggies and sprinkle with sea salt flakes, especially inside the potatoes and onion.

Place under the broiler for 8 minutes, or until the butter has melted and the vegetables are beginning to brown. If your broiler isn't particularly powerful, use a blowtorch to get a bit more color.

Transfer the vegetables and any liquid from the pan to a platter. Spoon over the reserved roasting juices.

Mix the lime juice, maple syrup and Worcestershire sauce together in a small bowl, then spoon evenly over the vegetables. Generously grate nutmeg and habanero over the top, sprinkle over some garam masala and serve with yogurt or sour cream.

See page 92 for a recipe photo. →

Plantains with chile honey butter

This is a really simple way of cooking plantain and yields delicious results, but you do have to use very ripe plantains—they should be soft and black or nearly all black. This recipe won't work with green or underripe plantains.

If you don't want to get all three dairy products that's absolutely fine, just use a 50/50 mix of whichever two you'll get most use out of. If you're not using the feta, add some extra salt.

Serves 4	GF, V
Prep time: 5–10 minutes	
Cook time: 40–45 minutes	

4 extra ripe plantains (see intro)
olive oil
lime, to serve

Feta yogurt (see intro)

scant ½ cup (100 g) plain yogurt
3½ oz (100 g) feta
½ cup (100 g) ricotta
1 lime, to serve

Chile honey butter

3½ tbsp salted butter
2 red bird's-eye chiles, thinly sliced into rounds
1 garlic clove, smashed with the side of a knife
1 tbsp Aleppo pepper flakes/pul biber or regular chile flakes
⅛ tsp fine sea salt
a good grating of whole nutmeg
a good pinch of garam masala
2 tbsp honey (or maple/agave syrup)

Preheat the oven to 400°F (200°C). Line a baking pan with parchment paper.

Poke a few holes all over each plantain, then place them on the lined pan and bake for 35 minutes, or until the skin is completely black and the plantains are very soft.

Use the tip of a knife to split the plantains open lengthways, squeezing the ends to push out the flesh (see the photo on page 93). Brush with a little oil and return to the oven for 5 minutes.

Use a whisk to mix the yogurt, feta and ricotta together until relatively smooth.

Put all the chile honey butter ingredients—*except* the honey—into a medium saucepan. Place on low heat and gently cook until the butter melts. Remove from the heat, immediately add the honey, and swirl the pan so the honey melts into the butter with the residual heat.

Spoon some of the feta yogurt into each plantain, then drizzle over the chile honey butter.

Finish with more nutmeg and garam masala. Serve with lime.

See page 93 for a recipe photo. →

Left Page Roasted root vegetables with maple, lime & chile
Right Page Plantains with chile honey butter

Fried greens with charred red pepper pimenta

You could dip all sorts of things into this batter, from green veggies and herbs, to fish, chicken, shrimp or squid.

In this instance I've opted for a few of my favorite greens, but feel free to mix it up!

The idea for this dish came about when I first came across *peixinhos da horta* (a furry green leaf that sort of looks like a large sage leaf) at the fruit and vegetable market in Bairro Peixoto in Rio (the neighborhood my mom was born in). *Peixinhos da horta* translates to "little fish of the vegetable garden," because the leaf has a fishy taste and traditionally it's battered and fried. For the lack of *peixinhos da horta* outside of Brazil, I tried it out with large leaf spinach and then decided I wanted other textures and flavors to accompany it. The combination of cornstarch, chickpea flour and fine polenta in the batter is very untraditional but really delivers in flavor and crunch.

The charred red pepper pimenta is completely addictive and versatile; use it as you would hot sauce.

Serves 4 as an appetizer   GF, V, VG
Prep time: 10 minutes
Cook time: 22–27 minutes

- 4 oz (120 g) okra, halved lengthways
- 2½ oz (70 g) large leaf spinach, stalks trimmed
- 2½ oz (70 g) scallions, green ends sliced 4 in (10 cm) long (use the whites in another recipe)
- 1 oz (30 g) cilantro sprigs
- about 4½ cups (900 g) light olive oil, for frying
- sea salt flakes
- 2 limes, halved, to serve

Charred red pepper pimenta

- 4 red romano peppers
- 1 Scotch bonnet chile
- 2 small garlic cloves, peeled
- 3 tbsp rice vinegar
- 2 tbsp olive oil
- ½ tsp fine sea salt
- 20 twists of freshly cracked pepper (⅛ tsp)

Batter

- ⅔ cup (150 g) cold sparkling water
- ⅔ cup (75 g) cornstarch
- ⅔ cup (60 g) chickpea flour
- ⅓ cup (60 g) fine polenta
- 1 tsp medium curry powder
- ¾ tsp fine sea salt
- plenty of freshly cracked pepper

Turn the oven to the highest broiler setting. Place the peppers and Scotch bonnet on a baking pan and broil for 7–10 minutes, or until blackened in patches. Remove the Scotch bonnet, turn the peppers over and broil for another 5–7 minutes, until softened and blackened in patches on the other side.

Let the peppers and Scotch bonnet cool for a few minutes, then remove the seeds and stalks. Keep the blackened skin on, as it adds flavor. Transfer the deseeded peppers and Scotch bonnet to a blender with all the remaining pimenta ingredients. Blend until smooth, then taste and adjust the seasoning. Depending on the size and sweetness of your peppers, you may need to add some extra salt, vinegar or a bit of honey.

Prep the veggies and herbs. Put the oil into a large pot and place on medium heat.

Put all the batter ingredients into a bowl and whisk until smooth.

Line a tray with paper towels.

Test if the oil is hot enough, either with a thermometer (you're after 350°F/180°C) or by dropping in a little of the batter, which should sizzle immediately.

Dip the greens into the batter, then scrape any excess batter off on the side of the bowl—they should be coated but not dripping too much. Carefully lower the greens into the hot oil and fry, stirring often, until crisp and golden brown. See below for timings and start with the herbs and spinach, which stay crunchier for longer.

Cilantro and spinach: about 1 minute.

Okra and scallion green ends: 1½–2 minutes.

Sprinkle with sea salt flakes and serve with the red pepper pimenta and with plenty of lime squeezed on top.

Egg, tomato & greens soup

Caldo de ovos (egg soup) is a dish with many different variations around the world, united by the use of cheap, easy, nutritious ingredients and often served to cure colds and hangovers.

The Brazilian version of egg drop soup is sometimes called *caldo de cabeça de galo* (rooster head soup), even though it doesn't actually contain rooster head! I assume it has something to do with the resemblance of the stringy ribbons of egg in the soup to a rooster's comb, although I may be wrong.

The Chinese version of egg drop soup is probably the most well-known; it features tomatoes and scallions in the base, cornstarch as a thickener and, of course, egg.

Caldo de ovos often contains spices like cumin or urucum (see page 23) in the base, has coarse cassava flour or *fubá* (cornmeal) as a thickener and is finished with *couve* (a cabbage variety similar to collard greens). I've also come across recipes that contain saffron and Worcestershire sauce, which I've added here too.

If you need an extremely easy and nourishing dinner within 15 minutes, look no further.

Serves 4 — GFO, V
Prep time: 10 minutes
Cook time: 20–23 minutes

Soup base

3 tbsp olive oil, plus extra for serving
2 very ripe tomatoes, roughly chopped (12 oz/320 g)
1½ oz (40 g) scallions, white ends finely chopped (save the green ends to serve)
1 tsp ginger–garlic mix (page 26), or 1 small garlic clove and ⅛ oz (4 g) fresh ginger, peeled and grated/crushed
½ Scotch bonnet chile, finely chopped (more/less depending on how much heat you like)
2¼ tsp fine sea salt
¾ tsp tomato paste
½ tsp ground urucum (aka annatto/achiote, see page 23) or ¼ tsp sweet paprika
¼ tsp ground cumin
a good pinch of saffron threads
plenty of freshly cracked pepper

Everything else

2 cups (500 g) chicken bone broth or vegetable stock (optional—you can use water)
2 tsp Worcestershire sauce or tamari
3½ tbsp coarse cassava flour or fine polenta
3 large eggs
1¾ oz (50 g) chard leaves, thinly sliced (or collard greens, cabbage, watercress)
sea salt flakes
1 lemon, halved

Put all the soup base ingredients into a large pot off the heat. Place on medium–low heat and gently stir-fry until the tomatoes are very soft, about 10–12 minutes.

Cover with 4¼ cups (1 liter) of water and the bone broth or stock (or omit and use 6⅓ cups/1.5 liters of water in total). Add the Worcestershire sauce.

Once simmering, slowly sprinkle in the cassava/polenta and whisk for 4–5 minutes until slightly thickened.

Whisk the eggs together in a bowl.

Create a vortex in the middle of the simmering soup with a large spoon, then add the egg mix in batches, about one-third at a time. Once you've poured each batch in, wait about 10 seconds before stirring, to achieve thin ribbons of cooked egg.

Turn off the heat and stir in the chard. Slice the scallion green ends and scatter them over. Drizzle with oil and finish with sea salt flakes. Squeeze over plenty of fresh lemon juice and serve.

Black-eyed pea cakes with toasted coconut salsa

These are inspired by *abará* and *acarajé*, two Afro-Bahian dishes made from peeled black-eyed peas *(feijão fradinho)*, onions and *dendê*. *Abará*, which includes dried shrimp and peanuts, is steamed in banana leaves, while *acarajé* is deep-fried in *dendê*. This version uses canned black-eyed peas and swaps peanuts for coconut. Masa harina, though untraditional, adds a lovely corn-y flavor, but chickpea or all-purpose flour would also work. These are a perfect party snack!

Makes 16 cakes	GF, V, VGO
Prep time: 15 minutes	
Cook time: 15 minutes	

Black-eyed pea cakes

- 1 × 14 oz (400 g) can of black-eyed peas, drained
- 2½ oz (70 g) yellow onion (1 small onion), chopped
- ½ cup (40 g) masa harina (or regular/chickpea flour)
- 3 tbsp red palm oil (see page 20)
- ½ cup (30 g) dried coconut flakes
- 2 tbsp tomato paste
- ¾ oz (20 g) ginger–garlic mix (page 26) or ⅓ oz (10 g) garlic and ⅓ oz (10 g) fresh ginger, peeled and very finely chopped
- ½ tsp medium curry powder
- ½ tsp fine sea salt
- ¼ tsp ground cinnamon
- a good grating of nutmeg
- plenty of freshly cracked pepper

Salsa

- 5¼ oz (150 g) ripe tomato, finely chopped
- ⅛ oz (5 g) cilantro, finely chopped
- 2 green bird's-eye chiles, thinly sliced into rounds
- 2 tbsp lime juice
- 1 tbsp olive oil
- 1 tsp rice vinegar
- 1 tsp ginger–garlic mix (page 26) or 1 small garlic clove and ⅛ oz (3 g) fresh ginger, peeled and very finely chopped
- ½ tsp honey (or maple/agave syrup)
- ¼ tsp ground cinnamon
- ¼ tsp fine sea salt

Toasted coconut

- 1¼ cups (50 g) dried coconut flakes
- 1 tbsp olive oil
- ¼ tsp fine sea salt

To serve

- coconut or regular yogurt
- 2 limes, cut into cheeks

Put all the ingredients for the cakes into a food processor and blend until smooth, scraping down the sides as needed.

With lightly oiled hands, form the mixture into 16 little patties weighing 1 oz (25 g) each.

Mix the salsa ingredients together in a small bowl.

For the toasted coconut, put the coconut flakes, olive oil and fine salt into a frying pan and place on medium–high heat. Cook for 2½–3 minutes, stirring every now and then, until the coconut flakes are golden brown and nicely toasted—take care not to burn them. Tip them onto a plate.

Return the pan to medium heat and brush with a little oil. In batches, place the cakes in the pan, spaced apart, and fry for 2 minutes on each side, or until golden brown. Be gentle when turning them, as they'll be delicate.

Transfer to a platter and top each with a small spoonful of coconut yogurt and a small spoonful of the salsa (avoiding the liquid, so the cakes don't get soggy).

Finish with the toasted coconut flakes, squeeze over some lime juice and serve.

Corn pie with caramelized onions & green chile oil

This pie is similar to cornbread but much more moist, with a quiche-like, creamy texture. It's inspired by *pamonha de forno*—a baked version of *pamonha* (corn and coconut parcels steamed in corn husks) that includes cheese and eggs. Near the border with Paraguay, you might hear *pamonha de forno* referred to as *chipa guazú*, a very similar Paraguayan dish.

The caramelized onions are a lovely addition, but to keep things simple you can skip this step and just blend the batter, swirl in some of the green chile oil and bake.

Serves 8 — GF, V
Prep time: 5–10 minutes
Cook time: 52–54 minutes
Cool time: 1 hour

2 tbsp olive oil, plus extra for greasing
1 large yellow onion, peeled, halved and thinly sliced (5¼ oz/150 g)
½ tsp fine sea salt
1 lemon, halved

Batter

1 × 14 oz (400 g) can of full-fat coconut milk
3 large eggs
2 cups (350 g) frozen corn, defrosted
7 oz (200 g) feta
1¾ oz (50 g) Parmesan, grated
¼ cup (40 g) polenta
1½ tsp medium curry powder
1 tsp ginger–garlic mix (page 26), or 1 small garlic clove + ⅛ oz (3 g) fresh ginger
1 tsp baking powder
1 tsp fine sea salt
plenty of freshly cracked pepper

Green chile oil

½ cup (100 g) olive oil
2 oz (60 g) cilantro
¾ oz (20 g) fresh chives
½ oz (15 g) fresh basil
1–2 green chiles, roughly chopped
1 tsp ginger–garlic mix (page 26), or 1 small garlic clove + ⅛ oz (3 g) fresh ginger
½ tsp fine sea salt

Preheat the oven to 400°F (200°C).

Put the oil, onion and salt into a frying pan on medium–low heat. Gently fry until soft and golden brown, 12–14 minutes. Turn the heat down if the onion is burning or becoming crispy.

Put all the batter ingredients into a blender or food processor in the order they're listed—i.e. wet ingredients first—and blend until smooth, scraping down the sides/mixing if needed.

Line a 10 in (25 cm) square baking pan with parchment paper and grease with a little oil. Pour in the batter.

Wash the blender, then add all the green chile oil ingredients and pulse until finely chopped, scraping down the sides as needed.

Mix the fried onions with ½ cup (100 g) of the green chile oil. Spoon evenly on top of the batter, then gently swirl into the surface.

Bake for 20 minutes, then rotate the pan and bake for another 20 minutes. The pie should be golden brown on top but still quite soft beneath. Cool for *at least* 1 hour, ideally longer, before serving. The center will be soft and moist when it's fresh out of the oven but it will set as it cools, much like a quiche.

Stir the juice of a lemon into the rest of the green chile oil and serve alongside.

SEAFOOD

Crudo with grated tomatoes & curried onions

In my opinion, there's no better way to start a meal than with raw seafood, because it excites the appetite without filling you up. I've made this dish for many of my pop-ups and it always goes down a storm. The curried onions are a bit of a revelation and you'll want them on everything—I strongly suggest keeping a stash in the fridge at all times.

When serving seafood raw, I would always advise going to a fishmonger rather than a supermarket. What's safe to serve raw will always depend on seasonality, freshness and where you are in the world.

I love using red mullet when it's available. Sea bream, sea bass, tuna and scallops also work very well. Shout out to the best fishmonger in London—Dan Murray at Oeno Maris in Newington Green—who is serious about sourcing and always gives me the best advice.

Pictured opposite is another version of this crudo, using the golden vinaigrette from the leek dish on page 62.

Serves 4 — GF
Prep time: 10–12 minutes
Cook time: 25–30 minutes

- 12 oz (350 g) sea bream or red mullet fillets, fridge cold
- sea salt flakes
- 2 scallions, green ends julienned (use the whites in another recipe)
- 2 limes, cut into cheeks (see page 23), to serve

Curried onions

- 6 tbsp olive oil
- 10½ oz (300 g) yellow onions (2–3 onions), peeled and finely chopped
- 1 tsp fine sea salt
- 10½ tbsp (150 g) salted butter
- 1 tbsp maple syrup
- 1½ tsp medium curry powder
- ½ tsp Urfa pepper flakes
- 1 dried habanero, deseeded and finely chopped (or ½ tsp chipotle flakes)

Grated tomatoes

- 4 very ripe, red tomatoes (1 lb/500 g)
- 2 tsp chopped red chile condiment (page 29, or use a store-bought chile condiment)
- 1 garlic clove, finely grated/crushed
- 1½ tbsp lemon juice
- ½ tsp fine sea salt
- olive oil

For the curried onions, put 3½ tablespoons of oil, the onions and the salt into a medium pan and very, very slowly fry until soft and deeply caramelized, 25–30 minutes. Don't be tempted to turn the heat up to speed up the process or you'll end up with crispy onions.

Meanwhile, brown the butter. Put the butter into a medium pot and place on medium heat. Cook until the butter melts, begins to foam and becomes a deep, golden brown, about 8 minutes. Remove from the heat and don't strain—the solids have lots of flavor.

Add the 2 tablespoons of oil, the caramelized onions, maple syrup, curry powder, Urfa and habanero to the pot of butter, stir and set aside.

Halve the tomatoes and scoop out the seeds. Grate the tomatoes using the large holes of a box grater. Discard the skins and mix the pulp with the chile paste, garlic, lemon, salt and a drizzle of oil.

With a very sharp knife, slice the fish at an angle off the skin (you should have about 5 slices per person).

Gently warm the curried onion butter on low heat, just enough to melt it so it's not set—you don't want it to be hot.

Spoon some of the grated tomato onto a platter and top with slices of fish. Sprinkle the fish with sea salt flakes, then spoon over some of the onion butter.

Finish with the scallions and a good squeeze of lime juice. Serve immediately (since the butter will set as it cools), with lime cheeks on the side.

Note
Keep the fish well chilled to make it easier to slice. Serve as soon as you've plated, or the butter in the curried onions will begin to set.

Crab pamonha in banana leaves

I've never come across a savory *pamonha* (page 56) with seafood, which is what inspired me to create this version topped with crab. Traditionally, *pamonha* are wrapped in corn husks, but for ease I use precooked corn kernels (frozen and defrosted or canned and drained), which means that I don't have any corn husks. Instead I like to wrap my *pamonha* in banana leaves, which makes for beautiful presentation and also lends a subtle leafy flavor that I love. Banana leaves are available in some Asian and Caribbean markets, but if you can't get hold of them, just use parchment paper instead.

Makes 10 — GF
Prep time: 10–12 minutes
Cook time: 10 minutes

- 1 pack of banana leaves
- 2 tbsp chile–ginger tempero (page 30, or see note)
- 2 scallions, green ends julienned (use the whites in another recipe)
- 2 limes, to serve

Pamonha

- 3 cups (500 g) frozen corn kernels, defrosted
- ¾ cup (120 g) quick-cook polenta or cornmeal
- scant ½ cup (100 g) full-fat coconut milk (from a can, not a carton; mix well before measuring)
- 2 oz (60 g) yellow onion (about ½ an onion), peeled and roughly chopped
- 2 tbsp coconut oil, plus more for greasing
- 1 tsp fine sea salt
- ½ tsp baking powder
- ½ tsp ground cumin
- 40 twists of freshly cracked pepper (about ¼ tsp)

Crab topping

- 7 oz (200 g) picked white crab meat (chopped cooked shrimp would also work well)
- 1 ripe plum tomato, deseeded and finely chopped (3 oz/80 g)
- 2 tbsp coconut oil
- ⅛ oz (5 g) fresh chives, finely chopped
- zest of 1 lime
- 1 tsp tomato paste
- ¼ tsp fine sea salt
- 50 twists of freshly cracked pepper (¼ tsp)

Put all the ingredients for the pamonha into a food processor or blender and blend until smooth, scraping down the sides as needed.

Preheat the oven to 450°F (230°C). Place a baking dish half-filled with water in the bottom of the oven to create steam. Have ready a large, flat baking sheet.

Cut ten (5½ × 6½ in/14 × 16.5 cm) rectangles out of banana leaves or parchment paper. If using the banana leaves, wipe both sides with a damp cloth. Lightly brush the leaves/paper with oil.

Spoon 3 oz (80 g) of the pamonha mixture into the center of each banana leaf/paper. Use your hands to form into a 2½ × 3 in (6 × 8 cm) rectangle. Brush the surface of the pamonha with a little oil.

Fold the two longer sides of the banana leaf together to enclose the pamonha on either side (as per the photo on page 58). Place on the baking sheet, seam side up, while you continue with the rest. Once all the pamonha are formed, bake for 10 minutes, until just set, then set aside to cool for a few minutes.

While the pamonha are baking, put all the crab ingredients into a pan along with the chile–ginger tempero (see note). Mix together, place on low heat and gently warm for 2 minutes.

Transfer the pamonha to a serving plate and open them. Top with a spoonful of the crab mixture and some sliced scallions. Squeeze over plenty of lime and serve while hot.

Note
If you don't want to make the chile–ginger tempero, add the following to the crab mixture instead: 1 very finely chopped red chile, ½ a crushed garlic clove, ⅓ oz (10 g) grated ginger and 1 tsp rice vinegar.

THE AMAZON AND KENRICK

The Amazon rainforest, "the lungs of the earth," is vast—more than twenty-eight times the size of the UK—and accounts for 60% of the world's remaining tropical rainforests. Nearly 60% of the Amazon is in Brazil and this area stretches across the states of Acre, Amapá, Amazonas, Maranhão, Mato Grosso, Pará, Rondônia, Roraima and Tocantins.

The Amazon river has seventeen major rivers flowing into it, including the Rio Negro and the Rio Solimões, which meet near Manaus (the capital of the state of Amazonas) in a beautiful phenomenon called Encontro das Águas (meeting of the waters). For several miles, the glassy black waters of the Rio Negro and the muddy, red-brown waters of the Rio Solimões flow side by side without mixing, due to differences in speed, temperature and density. It's an incredible thing to see from the plane as you fly into Manaus.

I first went to Manaus with my sister when I was seventeen, but I ended up in a dengue-induced fever dream for a week and didn't see much more than the hotel room ceiling. The second time I went (fifteen years later, with my best friend Romã) was more of a success. First, I didn't get dengue, and second, we had the good fortune of meeting the incredible Kenrick, a guide at the jungle lodge we stayed at. We were awed by his savviness and his wisdom—his knowledge not only of the Amazon but of the world—and we knew we needed his expertise for the book shoot.

Cut to Manaus the following year, with Kenrick as our local fixer. The very first place we shot was the Terminal Pesqueiro, the wholesale distribution point where fishermen from around the region bring their catch to sell to retailers. The Terminal Pesqueiro is not a public market and lies beyond the *linha vermelha* (red line), which is a metaphorical security boundary separating areas with high levels of violence in Brazil. Law enforcement and gangs are often in conflict in these areas and therefore movement is restricted, so if you're ever venturing beyond the *linha vermelha*, it's best to do so with a local who knows the lay of the land. I'm incredibly grateful to Kenrick for giving us access to this market, where we met fascinating characters who have spent their lives working in the Amazonian fishing trade. The Terminal Pesqueiro is one of the most exhilarating and hectic places I've ever been, the noise, smells and heat an assault on the senses in the very best possible way. The pictures on page 140 and 152 capture some of this action.

Kenrick Lacruz (or Papa Kenrick, as we lovingly dubbed him) is one of the most fascinating people I've ever met. The epitome of *fusão,* his mother was from the Wapishana tribe of the state of Roraima and his father was Guyanese, of Indian origin. Kenrick was "*nascido e criado na selva*" (born and raised in the jungle) in his mother's tribe and thus learned survival skills from a very young age, many of which he demonstrated to us during our time together.

From the bustle of the markets and ports of Manaus, we ventured to Kenrick's jungle home in the municipality of Manacapuru. We first drove over the Ponte Rio Negro, one of the longest bridges in Brazil, from which you can see jaw-dropping views of the mighty Rio Negro and the surrounding rainforest. From here we drove a couple of hours, first on tarmacked roads and then down a long dirt track that ended quite abruptly at the mouth of a small river. Here we were met by Clóvis, Kenrick's father-in-law, who helped load our luggage onto small speedboats to continue the journey on water. We sped through the *igarapé* (waterways) of the Rio Negro, through mangroves and around spectacular trees half-submerged in the glassy black waters.

As we traveled, Kenrick explained that the journey to his house—and life in the jungle itself—is very much dictated by two distinct seasons: the *seca* and the *cheia*. During the *seca* (dry) season, the waterways lower, exposing stretches of land that transform into earthy or sandy beaches. Local communities adapt, fishing in shallower waters and sowing crops like cassava, corn, beans and rice in the newly revealed *várzeas* (floodplains). Some *igarapé* dry up completely, making locations (like Kenrick's house) inaccessible by boat during that period.

During the *cheia* (full/flood) season, heavy rains flood the land, swelling the rivers and filling floodplains. Nutrients are washed back into the previously dry soil, giving way to a spectacular array of flora and fauna. The rivers teem with fish and the jungle comes back to life.

Seafood

We arrived at Kenrick's house in the middle of the jungle and somewhere in the middle of these two seasons. We were greeted by his beautiful family: his wife Rosa, his son Kenrick Junior, his daughter Natasha and their friends. They had assembled a plethora of Amazonian fish to cook for us. *Tambaqui, pirarucu, tucunaré, jaraquí, pintado, dourada, piranha* and *bodó* (see notes opposite), in all their curious shapes, sizes and colors, glistened in the sunlight as Kenrick explained the different ways to prepare each fish. On page 112 you can see that he prepares *piranha* by cutting a series of close diagonal slits along each side, a technique that cuts through its tiny bones, making it easier to eat.

As if that wasn't enough, Kenrick, his father-in-law and their friends built all the structures needed to cook this feast from scratch. Everything was "*feito na hora*"—made on the spot—in front of us. They cut down bamboo with machetes and constructed an intricate grill with a canopy of large palm leaves atop it to shield the fire. From bamboo and palm they also constructed a table, benches and a large, shaded gazebo from which they hung hammocks. They whittled spoons and knives and constructed cages to grill the fish in, they wove fans to protect us from the heat. All in less than an hour while we watched in awe!

A short boat ride away from the house is Kenrick's farm, where we hopped over to collect banana leaves, *malagueta* chiles and sugarcane stalks to cook with. Back at the house, Kenrick prepared the fish, rubbing them with lime juice and salt mixed with *urucum* (the seeds of a peppery red berry also known as annatto or achiote). The fish all got the same marinade—so the flavor of the fish and the aroma of the Amazonian wood could shine—but were prepared differently. He wrapped some in banana leaves, sewing the sides with the stringy fibers of a nearby palm tree. Some he grilled in cages and some he skewered over the fire.

When I asked Kenrick if he was proud to be Brazilian he responded, *"Tenho orgulho de ser indígena"*—"I am proud to be Indigenous"—and rightly so. It was inspiring to get to know someone with such strength and power (by the end of our time with Kenrick we were convinced he knew how to do everything and that he could surely fight off jaguars and crocodiles if needed) and yet with so much gentle humility.

My eternal thanks to Kenrick for going above and beyond for us and for teaching us the ways of his world, and to Rosa, Clóvis, Natasha, Kenrick Junior and their friends for their warmth and hospitality.

Notes:

Tambaqui: a large freshwater fish known for its rich, fatty meat.
Pirarucu: also known as *arapaima*. One of the largest freshwater fish in the world, reaching up to three metres in length.
Tucunaré: known as peacock bass because of its distinctive markings, which resemble the eyes on peacocks' feathers.
Jaraquí: known for its flavorful, oily flesh and for Kenrick's favorite saying, "*Quem come jaraqui não sai daqui,*" which means "Whoever eats jaraqui doesn't leave here."
Pintado: known as spotted catfish because of its spotted skin pattern.
Dourada: known as gilded catfish because of its golden-colored body.
Piranha: known for their sharp teeth and carnivorous diet.
Bodó: known as armored catfish because of its bony plates, which act as a protective shell. This fish looks like a robot or a transformer—truly one of the strangest creatures I've ever seen.

Flowers stuffed with shrimp & cod

Cooking with flowers (zucchini, squash, pumpkin) is something you're much more likely to come across in Italy or Mexico, but with the strong Italian influence in Brazil, you'll find flowers in some grocery stores and markets during the right season.

The filling here is inspired by the flavors of *bolinhos de bacalhau*—salt cod fritters, which originate in Portugal but are ubiquitous in almost every Brazilian café and restaurant. They are an essential addition to any good party—my family parties are never without a tray of *bolinhos*. I originally used salt cod in this recipe but found that it was a bit of a fuss to prepare, as it needs to be soaked and drained many times, so here I'm using quickly cured fresh cod as well as shrimp.

Another great version of this dish, if you can't get any flowers, is to stuff the mixture inside grilled baby peppers. To do this, turn the oven to the highest broiler setting. Place the peppers on a pan and broil for 7 minutes. Cut a slit in the side, deseed and pat dry, then fill with the mixture and heat in a 475°F (240°C) oven for 5 minutes.

Makes 16   **GF**
Prep time: 15 minutes
Cook time: 6–8 minutes

- 16 zucchini or squash flowers
- 1½ tbsp olive oil
- 1 ripe tomato (4½ oz/130 g), grated, skin discarded
- ½ a lemon
- sea salt flakes
- 1 lime, to serve

Shrimp oil

- 10½ oz (300 g) shell-on shrimp
- scant 1 cup (180 g) olive oil
- 3½ tbsp tomato paste
- 2 tbsp red palm oil (or use olive oil again)
- 1 Scotch bonnet chile
- 3 garlic cloves, crushed with the side of a knife
- 2 tsp Aleppo pepper flakes/pul biber
- ½ tsp fine sea salt
- ¼ tsp sweet paprika

Filling

- 10½ oz (300 g) cod, skin and pin-bones removed
- ⅓ oz (10 g) fresh chives, roughly chopped
- ⅛ oz (5 g) cilantro, roughly chopped
- 2 garlic cloves, peeled and roughly chopped
- 1 large egg
- zest of 1 lemon
- 1 red chile, finely chopped
- about 40 twists of freshly cracked pepper (¼ tsp)
- ¾ tsp fine sea salt

See page 118 for a recipe photo. →

Make the shrimp oil. Peel the shrimp, putting the heads and shells into a medium sauté pan off the heat. Devein the shrimp and set aside to use in the filling.

Add all the remaining shrimp oil ingredients to the pan of shells and heads. Place on medium heat and stir-fry for 5 minutes, until the heads turn from grey to bright pink. Use a spoon to mash everything together and release the flavors.

Place a colander over a saucepan, then spoon the shrimp shells and oil into the colander. Place a heavy bowl on top of the shells to squash them down—you want to extract as much of the liquid as possible, so push down hard a few times! Leave to strain while you prepare the flowers. Later, discard the shells and heads, then finely chop the Scotch bonnet and add to the oil.

Put the peeled shrimp into a food processor with all the filling ingredients. Pulse until very finely chopped, scraping down the sides as needed. Transfer to a pastry bag and cut the tip to get a ¾ in (2 cm) wide opening.

One at a time, gently open a flower and pipe in the filling. Use the natural stickiness of the filling to help seal the flower, twisting the top a little to keep it intact. Continue until all the flowers are filled.

Place a large frying pan on medium heat with the olive oil. Once the pan is hot, add the flowers, spaced apart, and fry for 4 minutes or until lightly browned. Gently turn them over and fry until nicely browned on the other side, 2–4 minutes.

Place the pan of shrimp oil on medium heat to warm through for a few minutes. Remove from the heat and stir in the grated tomato and the juice of ½ a lemon.

Transfer the flowers to a platter and spoon over the shrimp oil. Sprinkle with sea salt flakes and serve with fresh lime.

Note
If you don't have a food processor, finely chop the shrimp, cod, herbs and garlic by hand, then mix with the rest of the filling ingredients.

Moqueca fish burgers

Moqueca is a traditional *Bahian* seafood stew made with *azeite de dendê* (red palm fruit oil, see page 20), bell peppers and coconut milk. This burger is inspired by it, with more than a few untraditional twists: the sauce is smooth rather than textured and is made from all the ingredients that would usually go into the stew. I've added some spices (which are not Brazilian in origin but are nonetheless ubiquitous in Brazilian cuisine), and I've reimagined the dish as a burger (it's traditionally served with rice and salad).

This burger is intentionally saucy; I encourage you to serve it alongside a bowl of the sauce to dip your burger into as you go.

Serves 4

Prep time: 5–10 minutes

Cook time: 30 minutes

Marinade time: 30 minutes–1 hour

Rest time: 10 minutes

4 × 5¼ oz (150 g) skinless fish fillets (hake, haddock or cod would all work well)

2 tbsp olive oil

½ tsp fine salt

4 brioche burger buns

Moqueca sauce

1 × 14 oz (400 g) can of full-fat coconut milk

5¼ oz (150 g) sweet cherry tomatoes

1 red or yellow bell pepper, deseeded and quartered (6 oz/170 g)

½ a small yellow onion, peeled and roughly chopped (1¾ oz/50 g)

3 small garlic cloves, peeled

1 Scotch bonnet chile, deseeded (or a milder chile if you prefer)

3½ tbsp red palm oil (or use ghee or coconut oil + 1 tsp sweet paprika instead)

2 tbsp honey (or maple/agave syrup)

1¼ tsp fine sea salt

½ tsp medium curry powder

¼ tsp smoked paprika

¼ tsp ground turmeric

about 50 twists of freshly cracked pepper (¼ tsp)

Slaw

6½ oz (180 g) green cabbage, sliced on a mandoline

1½ oz (40 g) scallion green ends, thinly sliced into rounds (use the whites in another recipe)

2 green chiles, thinly sliced into rounds (optional)

2 tbsp kewpie mayo (or another mayo)

juice of 1 lime, plus extra to serve

¾ tsp fine sea salt

Put the fish fillets into a 9 × 12 in (23 × 30 cm) roasting pan and season with the oil and salt. Mix to coat.

Put all the ingredients for the moqueca sauce into a blender and blend until completely smooth. Pour into the pan of fish and mix to coat all the fillets in sauce. Leave to marinate for 30 minutes to 1 hour at room temperature.

Preheat the oven to 500°F (260°C), or as high as your oven will go. Once the oven is hot, bake for 30 minutes, or until the sauce is bubbling and has reduced and thickened somewhat. Set aside to cool while you toast the buns.

Halve the buns and toast both sides in a very hot pan until golden brown.

Mix all the ingredients for the slaw together.

Place a fish fillet on the bottom of each bun and spoon over plenty of sauce. Top with a generous amount of slaw and the other half of the bun. Serve at once, with a bowl of sauce alongside to dip into and some extra lime.

Tuna & cassava in a ginger, tomato & lime broth

This soup is inspired by the Ecuadorian dish *encebollado*—specifically the one made at El Inca Plebeyo, one of my favorite London restaurants, run by chef Jorge Pacheco and his lovely family. *Encebollado* means "with onions" and this stew traditionally features tuna and cassava in a broth flavored with onions and topped with pickled onions.

Incidentally, Ecuador is one of the few countries in South America that *doesn't* border Brazil; however, I have no problem including my version of this recipe in the book because all these ingredients—cassava, tuna, lime—are used in Brazilian cuisine and the combination is one that any Brazilian would love.

This version is much more tomato-y and less onion-y than the traditional, and also includes lots of fresh ginger and lime in the broth. I like to serve a big plate of freshly washed, still-wet herbs on the side, reminiscent of the plate of herbs you'd get with a pho, for people to add as they please.

Serves 4	GF
Prep time: 10 minutes	
Cook time: 22–34 minutes	
Cure time: 30–40 minutes	

1 lb (500 g) raw tuna, cut into 2 in (5 cm) chunks (or use another fish if you like)
1 tsp fine sea salt
1 lb (500 g) fresh cassava root

Broth

4 tbsp tomato paste
3 tbsp olive oil
⅓ oz (10 g) fresh ginger, peeled and julienned
1 garlic clove, finely grated/crushed
1 Scotch bonnet chile or 3 piri piri chiles
2¼ tsp sea salt flakes
plenty of freshly cracked pepper
½ tsp rice (or another) vinegar
½ tsp honey (or maple/agave syrup)

Toppings

2 green chiles, thinly sliced into rounds
½ oz (15 g) scallion green ends, julienned (use the whites in another recipe)
½ a yellow onion, peeled and thinly sliced
⅓ oz (10 g) cilantro
⅓ oz (10 g) fresh basil
1 lime, halved, plus more to serve

Put the tuna into a bowl with the fine sea salt, mix and set aside to lightly cure at room temp for up to 1 hour.

Prep the cassava—peel away the thick brown skin as well as the pinkish layer beneath and remove any soft or blackened parts. Cut into 2½ in (6 cm) long cylinders, then halve lengthways. Remove the hard fiber running through the middle by pulling it out or with a knife. Add to a bowl of water as you go to prevent discoloration.

Put the prepped cassava into a large pot with plenty of salted cold water. Place on medium-low heat, cover with a lid and cook until very soft all the way through, 20–30 minutes. Turn off the heat and leave in the water.

While the cassava is cooking, in a separate large pot off the heat, make the broth. Put the tomato paste, oil, ginger, garlic, Scotch bonnet, salt and pepper into the pot. Place on medium heat and stir-fry for 3 minutes.

Add the vinegar, honey and 5¼ cups (1.25 liters) of water and bring to a gentle simmer.

Drain the cassava and add to the broth along with the tuna. Cook for 3–4 minutes, or until the tuna is *just* cooked through and a little pink inside (or longer if you prefer).

Prepare a platter with all the toppings.

Squeeze the juice of a lime into the stew and serve with the fresh herbs and more lime.

Notes

If you can't find cassava, use golden sweet potatoes or regular potatoes (you won't need to boil them as long as cassava).

I like to use a relatively fatty cut of tuna for this. You can swap the tuna for other fish and/or shrimp, if you like.

AZEITE DE DENDÊ

My first introduction to *azeite de dendê* (red palm oil) was at a restaurant on Ponta Negra beach in Natal, where my mom's family is from. I was young but I remember it clearly; as a clay pot of bubbling *moqueca* was lowered onto our table, I noticed cosmic patterns on the surface of the steaming stew. What I first thought was oil reddened by tomato and spices was actually a sacred ingredient I'd never heard of and the start of an obsession.

Azeite de dendê is an oil made from red palm fruit. It has a vibrant color—my favorite color in fact—which I like to describe as "burning tangerine sunset" and a flavor that really has to be tasted to be understood. It has the texture of ghee when set, with notes of butter, carrot and paprika. It's savory without being salty, and in my opinion it has the most complex flavor profile of any plant-based fat. It's a truly wondrous ingredient; in its raw form it's rich with antioxidants, beta-carotenes and vitamins A and E, which promote healthy brain and heart function. I love its unique flavor and use it in many recipes throughout the book.

Native to West Africa, *dendê* was taken to Brazil during the transatlantic slave trade. A staggering 4.9 million enslaved Africans were forcibly taken to Brazil during this time (more than any other country in the world), and the majority were taken in through Salvador, the port of Bahia. *Dendê* took to the climate incredibly well, and *dendezeiros* (red palm fruit trees) now form a landscape stretching 4½ miles (115 km) from Salvador, known as the Costa do Dendê (the *dendê* coast).

Dendê (from the Kimbundu language spoken in Angola) is now ubiquitous in Brazil and a cornerstone of Afro-Brazilian culture; a physical reminder of the ways in which African soul enriched Brazil, despite horrendous circumstances. *Dendê* is integral in Bahian dishes like *moqueca, vatapá* and *caruru.* It's also used in Candomblé, a religion created in the nineteenth century by Afro-Brazilians as a *fusão* of Yoruba, Bantu and Fon traditions with Catholicism. In Candomblé, *dendê* is considered to be the physical manifestation of "*axé*," from the Yoruba meaning "life force, divine power, essence of being or existence."

Then there's the refined, bleached version of palm oil, the product of toxic monoculture used in everything from Nutella to conditioner. This is the version that has had devastating implications for the environment and for wildlife. The other tragedy—and I don't use that word lightly—is that this has led to the demonization of the sacred *dendê*, despite the fact that West Africans and Afro-Brazilians have been using red palm oil for thousands or hundreds of years respectively and farming it regeneratively and ethically all the way.

Whenever I publish a recipe including red palm oil I always get backlash to the tune of, "*I can't believe you're promoting palm oil, disappointing!*" and it irks me because those commenting have no idea what they're talking about. I couldn't put it better than Joshua Kwaku Asiedu, a Ghanaian organic farmer who posted the following on Instagram on 11 June 2022: "*. . . when white Europeans colonized* most of the world, they found lots of marvelous resources, which combined with that toxic mindset of massive/greedy production, ended up planting palm trees . . . all around their colonies, creating toxic monoculture, destroying natural forests and killing important species of our planet. The point here is that most people (who are) against palm oil are the fore-children of the same colonizers, blaming on this marvelous Indigenous tree, instead of pointing at the original polluted system from where most are still benefiting."

To summarize, it's not palm oil that's the problem, it's the over-commercialization of refined palm oil for the benefit of the developed world and the toxic monoculture that this has created.

SILVIO

My obsession with *dendê* and my desire to see the way it's traditionally made brought us to Silvio, who produces "*dendê de pilão*"—red palm oil artisanally made using a large pestle (*pilão*)—in the community of Cova da Onça, a village on the island of Boipeba in the Cairu archipelago of Bahia.

Getting there was quite a journey. First, we got a ferry from Salvador to Itaparica. We then drove down the coast along scenic roads flanked by cacao trees and dizzyingly tall *palmeiras*. After a few hours, the tarmac morphed into a brick-red dirt track so astonishingly pigmented we had to clamber off the van just to marvel at the wonder of it. We followed this track for a while, passing a soccer field, seemingly in the middle of nowhere, with faded pink spectator stands and white herons lazing on the waterlogged grass in the afternoon sun (see pages 242–243). Just past the field was Carvalho, from where we took a boat over to Cova da Onça, passing tiny islands surrounded by mangroves.

Cova da Onça (which means jaguar's cave) is completely unspoiled, with no cars or infrastructure and with streets of sand. As we walked through the beachside community we passed an older man hand-sewing a fishing net that stretched across the front of his house, and he explained that it took two weeks of very concentrated work to sew a net that size. We passed another house with large fillets of fish salt-curing in the sun and lobster cages—empty but full of promise—haphazardly piled against the wall. We passed the local *boteco* and saw that the guy running the bar was the same guy who'd just driven us over in the boat, illustrating the size of this beautiful little community.

Before taking us to his house for dinner, Silvio led us up the mountain to see the sunset. What greeted us at the summit after a forty-minute incline can only be described as a scene from the land before time, untouched nature as far as the eye could see—jungle flecked with tall palm trees and mangrove wetlands on one side and the glistening sea, wrapping itself around several small bays, on the other. The sun set as a full moon rose and Silvio explained the significance of this area, a refuge for descendants of enslaved African people.

The next day Silvio demonstrated how he makes *dendê*, the way his parents taught him when he was barely tall enough to hold the *pilão* (pestle). He started by scaling a dizzyingly tall *dendezeiro* (red palm fruit tree), using a steel and wood cable called a *peia de aço* that loops around one foot and the opposite thigh. We watched in wonder as he effortlessly climbed, lithely navigating around huge, sharp spines along the way, to hack a large *cacho* (bunch) of *dendê* with a machete from the very top.

Back down on terra firma, Silvio showed us the next steps, along with his sister América and his mother-in-law.

1. Remove the *dendê* fruits from the spiny *cacho (bunch)*.
2. Boil the *dendê* fruits to soften them.
3. Pound the *dendê* vigorously with the *pilão*.
4. Wash the pounded fruit, creating repeated vigorous motions in the water to dislodge the fat, which then rises to the top.
5. Scoop the fat into a separate vat.
6. Repeat the above processes until the vat is full of yellow, foamy fat.

The final step is to cook the fat over a wood fire, which turns it from a foamy, murky yellow to the most astonishing, vivid burning tangerine sunset color. For Silvio this is perhaps the most important part, because he cooks his oil with an extremely aromatic leaf plucked from a nearby bush. This secret ingredient, he explains, is what makes his *dendê* so good—and he's right, I've never tasted better *dendê*. To know that it's made with such care, preserving methods passed down from ancestors who experienced unimaginable hardship—and for whom this ingredient is sacred—makes it even more special.

I'm incredibly grateful to Silvio, his wife Dora (who makes the best *bolo de macaxeira* I've ever tasted) and his sister América for welcoming us into their home for a couple of days and looking after us as if we were family.

So, my final point is: buy sustainable red palm oil, experiment with this wondrous ingredient and support smallholder farmers and regenerative agriculture while you're at it. One day I hope to bring Silvio's inimitable *azeite de dendê* home with me, but until then, brands I recommend are Pure Indian Foods and Juka's Organic, available online.

Clam moqueca with cilantro & lime vinagrete

This is a take on *moqueca*, the classic Bahian stew traditionally made with fish and/or shrimp, coconut milk and dendê. Here, I use clams for a quick and delicious twist that pairs beautifully with the ginger–garlic–cilantro fries on page 70. For an extra special version, serve the clams over roasted plaice (see below for the recipe and overleaf for the photo).

Serves 4 — GF
Prep time: 5–10 minutes
Cook time: 16–17 minutes
Clam cleaning time: 1–2 hours

fine sea salt
1 lb 3 oz (1 kg) clams
2 tbsp red palm oil (or coconut oil + ½ tsp sweet paprika)
1 red/yellow bell pepper, finely chopped (4 oz/120 g)
4 garlic cloves, finely chopped (not crushed!)
1 red chile, finely chopped (deseeded if you like)
1 Scotch bonnet chile (whole)
5¼ oz (150 g) sweet, ripe cherry tomatoes, halved
2 tsp tomato paste
1¼ tsp sweet paprika
1 × 14 oz (400 g) can of full-fat coconut milk
1 lime, halved

Vinagrete

⅓ oz (10 g) yellow onion (1 slice), finely chopped
⅛ oz (5 g) fresh chives, finely chopped
⅛ oz (5 g) cilantro, finely chopped
3 tbsp olive oil
¼ tsp fine sea salt
juice of 1 lime

In a large bowl, mix 2 tablespoons of fine sea salt with plenty of cold water. Add the clams and leave for 1–2 hours, stirring every now and then. Rinse and drain to get rid of sand and grit and discard any broken clams.

Put the palm oil into a 12 in (30 cm) wide, high-sided pot and place on medium heat. Once melted, add the bell pepper, garlic, both chiles and 1 teaspoon of fine sea salt to the pot. Gently fry for 5 minutes, stirring often, until the peppers are beginning to soften and the garlic is fragrant. You don't want the garlic to brown, so turn the heat down if necessary.

Add the tomatoes, tomato paste and paprika. Stir-fry for 2 minutes, then stir in the coconut milk and simmer for 3 minutes. Add the clams to the pot in a single layer. Cover with a lid and turn the heat all the way down. Cook for 4–5 minutes, or until all the shells have opened. Discard any that remain closed.

Mix together all the ingredients for the vinagrete.

Squeeze the Scotch bonnet into the sauce if you like heat, or remove it if you prefer. Squeeze over plenty of lime juice.

Spoon over the vinagrete and serve.

Whole roasted plaice

Serve this with the clam moqueca (above) or simply roast with a Flavor Bomb (pages 24–31) to accompany. For smaller fish, 1 lb 12 oz (800 g) should take around 12 minutes and 1 lb (500 g) around 8 minutes.

Serves 4 — GF
Prep time: 2 minutes
Cure time: 30 minutes–1 hour
Cook time: 15–18 minutes

1 lb 3 oz (1 kg) plaice, with skin
fine sea salt
freshly cracked pepper
olive oil

See page 136 for a recipe photo. →

Pat the fish dry with paper towels. Sprinkle generously with fine sea salt and pepper, then rub all over with olive oil. Leave to lightly cure for 30 minutes to 1 hour at room temperature.

Preheat the oven to 475°F (240°C). Line a flat baking sheet with parchment paper. Put the plaice on the prepared pan and roast near the top of the oven for 15 minutes, or until the skin is crisp and lightly charred in places.

Finish under a hot broiler for a few minutes to get more color, or use a blowtorch if you have one.

Left Ginger-garlic-cilantro fries
Right Clam moqueca

Escondidinho de peixe com couve flor

Escondidinho (es-kon-jee-jee-nyo) translates to "little hidden one" and refers to a baked dish of meat or fish concealed under a layer of cassava purée. Traditionally the filling is mixed with cream or *requeijão* (a cream cheese that tastes a lot like Dairylea or Laughing Cow). The topping is made with cassava, puréed with serious amounts of butter, cream and grated cheese.

I often avoid *escondidinho* because it's too rich. In this lighter version I've swapped cassava for cauliflower and *requeijão* for coconut milk. It might sound virtuous, but trust me when I tell you it's completely delicious.

Serves 6 — GF
Prep time: 10–12 minutes
Cook time: 33–35 minutes
Rest time: 15 minutes

- 1 lb 5 oz (600 g) white fish, skin off and cut into 2 in (5 cm) chunks
- 6 oz (170 g) raw jumbo shrimp
- fine sea salt
- 1 × 14 oz (400 g) can of full-fat coconut milk (mix very well before measuring out)
- 1 tbsp lime juice
- 2½ tbsp quick-cook polenta or farofa

Filling
- 2 romano peppers, deseeded and sliced widthways into strips
- 1 yellow onion, peeled, halved and thinly sliced
- 3 garlic cloves, peeled and roughly chopped
- 3 tbsp coconut oil
- 2 tbsp tomato paste
- 1 Scotch bonnet chile
- 1 tsp medium curry powder
- 1 tsp fine sea salt
- 50 twists of freshly cracked pepper (¼ tsp)
- ½ tsp Aleppo pepper flakes
- ¼ tsp sweet paprika

Cauliflower purée
- 2 large cauliflowers, leaves removed, cut into florets
- 2 tbsp ghee (from a jar, not a can) or butter
- 2½ tsp English mustard
- 1¼ tsp fine sea salt
- 1 tsp rice (or another) vinegar
- 20 twists of freshly cracked pepper (⅛ tsp)
- a good grating of nutmeg

To finish
- olive oil
- 1 oz (30 g) Parmesan or another cheese

Put the fish and shrimp into a bowl with 1½ teaspoons of fine sea salt. Mix and set aside to lightly cure while you prepare the rest.

Put the cauliflower florets into a 12 in (30 cm) wide pot for which you have a lid. Pour in enough water to come 1½ in (4 cm) up the side of the pot. Place on medium heat, cover with a lid and cook for 18–20 minutes, or until the cauliflower is *very* soft all the way through. Don't worry if the water evaporates and the cauliflower on the bottom browns a bit, this adds extra flavor.

Meanwhile, put all the filling ingredients into a large ovenproof pot on medium heat (I use an 11 in/28 cm Dutch oven). Stir-fry for 9 minutes or until the onion is soft and golden, turning the heat down if the mixture starts to catch or burn.

Pour in three-quarters (1¼ cups/300 g) of the coconut milk (saving the rest for the purée), add the lime juice, then whisk in the polenta until the mixture thickens slightly, about 3 minutes. Squeeze the Scotch bonnet into the sauce (or remove it if you prefer less heat). Stir in the fish and shrimp, cook for 2 minutes, then turn off the heat.

Put the cooked cauliflower into a food processor or blender along with the remaining scant ½ cup (100 g) of coconut milk, the ghee, mustard, salt, vinegar, pepper and nutmeg. Blend until completely smooth, scraping down the sides as needed.

Preheat the oven to the highest broiler setting.

Cover the fish with the cauliflower purée—start by spooning the purée around the edges of the pot and then work your way in. Use the back of the spoon to create dips in the surface. Drizzle with olive oil, grate over the cheese, and bake near the top of the oven for 15 minutes, or until golden brown and bubbling. Use a blowtorch to get a bit more color on the surface, if you have one.

Leave to cool for 15 minutes before serving.

Roast mackerel with lime butter & green chile vinagrete

I feel like people are very often put off by cooking whole fish, but it really couldn't be quicker or easier. This mackerel dish comes together very quickly and the zingy green vinagrete perfectly cuts through the richness of the mackerel and the lime butter.

Serves 4 — GF
Prep time: 5–7 minutes
Cook time: 16–17 minutes

2 whole mackerel, gutted and cleaned (about 13 oz/380 g each)
fine sea salt
freshly cracked pepper
6 scallions, ends trimmed

Lime butter

4 tbsp (60 g) salted butter
1 tbsp olive oil
3 tbsp lime juice (1½ large limes)
⅓ oz (10 g) fresh ginger, peeled and thinly sliced
1 small garlic clove, grated/crushed
¼ tsp fine sea salt

Green chile vinagrete

2 green chiles, deseeded and finely chopped
⅓ oz (10 g) fresh chives, finely chopped
⅓ oz (10 g) cilantro, finely chopped
½ a small garlic clove, grated/crushed
3 tbsp olive oil
2 tsp rice vinegar
1 tsp sea salt flakes

Preheat the oven to 425°F (220°C).

With a sharp knife, score the skin of the mackerel diagonally at ¾ in (2 cm) intervals and place in a 9 × 13 in (24 × 34 cm) baking pan. Season the cavity of the fish generously with fine sea salt and pepper, then stuff with the scallions.

Place all the butter ingredients in a small pan and gently heat until the butter melts. Pour over and around the mackerel, then roast near the top of the oven for 10 minutes. Remove the pan from the oven and baste the fish very well. Turn the oven to the highest broiler setting and broil for 4–5 minutes, or until the skin is crisp and bubbling.

While the fish is cooking, put all the ingredients for the vinagrete into a small bowl and stir.

Transfer the mackerel and scallions to a platter along with the lime butter from the pan.

Spoon over some of the vinagrete and serve the rest alongside.

Tuna tartare with red pepper pimenta & batata palha

This makes an incredibly impressive appetizer. The *batata palha* (fried potato sticks) topping is completely optional but adds a lovely texture—I would highly recommend making them (page 31), otherwise use store-bought potato sticks.

The red pepper pimenta works really well as a dip, condiment or in sandwiches.

Serves 4 as an appetizer — GF
(not including batata palha)
Prep time: 5–10 minutes
Cook time: 12–17 minutes

14 oz (400 g) sashimi-grade tuna
batata palha (page 31), to serve (optional)
1–2 green bird's-eye chiles, thinly sliced
1 lime, to serve

Charred red pepper pimenta

4 red romano peppers
1 Scotch bonnet chile
2 large garlic cloves (¼ oz/8 g), peeled
2 tbsp olive oil
3 tbsp rice vinegar
½ tsp fine sea salt
20 twists of freshly cracked pepper (⅛ tsp)

Dressing

1¼ tbsp tamari or soy sauce
1¼ tbsp rice vinegar
1 tbsp maple syrup
1 tsp toasted sesame oil
⅛ tsp fine sea salt

If making the batata palha (page 31), do this first.

For the pimenta, turn the oven to the highest broiler setting. Place the peppers and Scotch bonnet on a baking pan and broil for 7–10 minutes, or until blackened in patches. Remove the Scotch bonnet, then turn the peppers over and grill for another 5–7 minutes, until softened and charred on the other side.

Leave to cool for a few minutes, then remove the seeds and stalks from the peppers and the Scotch bonnet. Place in a blender with the rest of the pimenta ingredients. Blend until completely smooth. Adjust the seasoning—you may want to add some salt, vinegar or honey depending on the size and flavor of your peppers.

Mix all the dressing ingredients together.

Cut the tuna into ½ in (1½ cm) cubes. Just before serving, add some of the dressing and toss to coat.

Spoon some of the pimenta onto a large plate (or plate individually) and top with the dressed tuna. Finish with the batata palha (if using—see intro) and green chiles, and serve with lime.

Shrimp, okra & mango juice stew

This dish is inspired by *caruru paraense,* a shrimp and okra stew with mixed Indigenous and African origins. It's popular in Bahia and is often associated with the religious rituals of Candomblé (page 124).

This version is very different to the original—it's much more brothy and uses mango juice and it doesn't contain palm oil or nuts. It's super speedy and simple, perfect for a midweek meal with some coconut rice.

Serves 4 — GF
Prep time: 5 minutes
Cook time: 5 minutes
Marinade time: 10 minutes

- 14 oz (400 g) peeled and deveined jumbo shrimp (1 lb 12 oz/800 g if starting with shell-on shrimp)
- 7 oz (200 g) okra, halved diagonally
- 2 bird's-eye chiles, thinly sliced into rounds, plus extra to serve
- 3 tbsp olive oil, plus extra for cooking
- 1 tsp fine sea salt
- 1½ tsp ground cumin
- ¼ tsp ground turmeric
- ¼ tsp ground cinnamon
- 15 saffron threads
- 60 twists of freshly cracked pepper (⅓ tsp)
- sea salt flakes
- 1 lime, halved

Broth

- 1¼ cups (300 g) mango juice (see note)
- 3½ tbsp water
- 2½ tbsp tomato paste
- 1½ tbsp ginger–garlic mix (page 26, or 1 large garlic clove + ⅓ oz (10 g) peeled fresh ginger + ⅛ tsp fine sea salt, very finely minced together)

Put the shrimp, okra and chiles into a large bowl with the oil, salt, spices, saffron and pepper. Mix and leave to marinate for 10 minutes.

In a separate bowl, whisk together the mango juice, water, tomato paste and ginger–garlic mix.

Lightly grease a 12 in (30 cm) sauté pan and place on high heat. Once hot, add the shrimp, okra and marinade, spread out as much as possible and fry undisturbed for 2 minutes, then stir-fry for another 30 seconds to 1 minute, or until the shrimp are all pink. Pour over the broth, cover with a lid and cook until the broth is just hot, 2–3 minutes. Don't overcook—you want the okra to remain vibrant and crunchy, and the shrimp juicy.

Squeeze over plenty of fresh lime and serve.

Note
Make sure you're using juice with no added sugar or fake flavorings. If you can't get pure mango juice, mango and apple juice would also work well, and pineapple juice would be a good alternative.

Grilled fish with mango curry butter

This recipe is ridiculously simple—easy enough for a midweek meal and impressive enough to serve at a dinner party.

The mango curry butter works in lots of different contexts; try rubbing it all over a spatchcocked chicken before roasting at 475°F (250°C) for 40 minutes, or melt it over grilled shrimp or roasted plantain. Try a variation with papaya jam instead of mango jam in the butter (page 27).

A smaller, 12 oz (350 g) plaice should take around 6 minutes. Fillets or steaks (cod or haddock, for example) weighing 7 oz (200 g) should also take around 6 minutes under the broiler.

Serves 2 — GF
Prep time: 5 minutes
Cook time: 9–11 minutes

2 × 1 lb (500 g) sole or plaice (see note)
olive oil
3 oz (80 g) scallions, green ends cut into 4 in (10 cm) lengths (use the whites in another recipe)
sea salt flakes
1 lime, to serve
1 lemon, to serve

Mango curry butter

7 tbsp (100 g) salted butter
3 tbsp mango jam (page 27, or use a store-bought mango chutney)
1 tbsp chopped red chile condiment (page 29), or use a store-bought chopped chile condiment)
2 tsp medium curry powder
2 garlic cloves, very finely chopped
⅛ oz (5 g) cilantro, very finely chopped
plenty of freshly cracked pepper

Put all the butter ingredients into a medium saucepan and place on medium–low heat. Gently cook until the butter has melted, 2–3 minutes, stir, then set aside to cool for a few minutes.

Preheat the oven broiler to the highest temperature.

Very lightly grease a baking sheet with olive oil—just enough so that the fish doesn't stick. Place the sole, skin side up and spaced apart, on the pan. Pat dry, then sprinkle generously and evenly with salt. Spoon the butter evenly over the fish, leaving some butter in the pan to finish the dish with.

Rinse the scallion green ends so they're slightly damp—this will stop them burning—then spread them out on top of the fish.

Broil on the top rack of the oven for 7–8 minutes, or until the fish is cooked through and the scallions are very lightly charred.

Transfer to a platter, sprinkle with sea salt flakes and spoon more of the mango butter over the fish (warm it first if it's set). Squeeze over plenty of fresh lime and lemon and serve.

Note
I like to use flat fish here like sole or plaice, which cook very quickly. The method here includes cooking time for a 1 lb (500 g) sole, trimmed to remove the head and fins.

Camarão na moranga

Camarão na moranga (kah-mah-rowng nah moh-rahn-gah)—literally "shrimp in pumpkin"—is a dish from Ubatuba, a town on the south-east coast of the state of São Paulo.

Traditionally shrimp are cooked in a sauce made with cream, *requeijão* (see page 139) and grated cheese, then cooked inside a whole roasted pumpkin or squash. I find the original to be *far* too rich and creamy, but I love the artistry of the presentation, so here I've come up with a much lighter coconut-based version.

I use kabocha squash, also sometimes known as a Japanese pumpkin. It's worth noting that in Japanese, kabocha simply means "pumpkin" or "squash"; however, outside of Japan the name refers to this particular variety.

Kabocha is incredibly nutty, sweet and creamy, perfect for this recipe. If you can't get kabocha, use another variety of a similar shape and size like Hokkaido, crown prince or delica pumpkin. Avoid stringy/watery varieties like spaghetti squash, field pumpkin, yellow squash and delicata squash.

Serves 4 — GF
Prep time: 5 minutes
Cook time: 1 hour 8–23 minutes
Marinade time: 20 minutes
Rest time: 10 minutes

3½ lb (1.6 kg) kabocha squash (see intro)
olive oil
fine sea salt
10½ oz (300 g) jumbo shrimp, peeled and deveined (1 lb 5 oz/600 g if starting with shell-on shrimp)
1 Scotch bonnet chile (optional)
1 × 14 oz (400 g) can of full-fat coconut milk
1 lime, to serve

Marinade

3 tbsp tomato paste
2 tbsp red palm oil (or ghee/coconut oil + ½ tsp sweet paprika)
1 tbsp olive oil
¾ tbsp onion powder
2 small garlic cloves, peeled and grated/crushed
1 tsp medium curry powder
¾ tsp fine sea salt
¾ tsp chile flakes
a good grating of nutmeg
plenty of freshly cracked pepper

Preheat the oven to 410°F (210°C).

Poke holes all over the squash with a fork and place it on a baking pan. Rub all over with oil and salt, then roast for 1 hour, or until the squash is soft and the skin has browned. This may take 10–15 minutes longer if your squash is bigger than 3½ lb (1.6 kg).

Meanwhile, combine all the marinade ingredients in a bowl. Add the shrimp and the Scotch bonnet, if using, mix to coat and leave to marinate for 20 minutes.

Heat a large sauté or frying pan on medium heat. Once hot, add the shrimp, Scotch bonnet and all the marinade from the bowl. Space the shrimp apart and fry for 2 minutes, then flip and fry for another 1 minute. Pour in the coconut milk and stir together. Gently simmer for 2 minutes, then remove from the heat. Squash the Scotch bonnet to release its flavor, then remove (or chop up and stir into the sauce if you like heat).

After 1 hour, remove the kabocha from the oven. Carefully (as it will be very hot), use a sharp knife to slice the very top off the squash, then scoop out the seeds. Set the lid aside, off the pan.

Preheat the broiler to its highest temperature.

Season the insides of the kabocha with a little salt, and use a spoon to compact the cooked flesh into the sides to create more room for the shrimp.

Carefully fill with the shrimp and sauce, then drizzle the surface evenly with a little oil. Broil for about 8 minutes, or until the surface is browned and bubbling.

Leave to cool for 10 minutes, then slice and serve with fresh lime. The lid will of course be edible as well!

Note
If your pumpkin splits while roasting, just wrap the outside tightly in foil before you spoon in the shrimp filling.

Scallop crudo with orange & burnt chile vinagrete

This impressive appetizer comes together in less than 10 minutes. I love the sweet, buttery flavor of raw scallops, but you can pan-fry them if you prefer. To do this, dry the scallops well and season generously with salt. Heat butter and olive oil in a nonstick frying pan on high heat and cook the scallops for 3 minutes on the first side, pressing down to form a golden brown crust, then for 1 minute on the other side.

The vinagrete pairs beautifully with all kinds of seafood—spoon it over oysters or serve it alongside grilled shrimp or fish.

And feel free to experiment with other sweet citrus in the vinagrete—tangerine, clementine, orange, blood orange, for example. Just make sure whatever you're using is sweet and ripe. When a dish contains so few ingredients it's incredibly important that those ingredients are of good quality, so avoid bland, underripe citrus.

Serves 4 — GF
Prep time: 5 minutes
Cook time: 5 minutes

- 1½ tbsp ghee (homemade or store-bought from a jar, not from a can) or salted butter
- 8 scallops, cleaned and roe removed
- sea salt flakes
- 1 lime, to serve

Orange vinagrete

- 1 Scotch bonnet chile
- 1 ripe, sweet orange
- 3 oz (80 g) sweet cherry tomatoes, deseeded and finely diced
- 1 oz (30 g) banana shallot, finely diced (about 1 medium)
- 1½ tbsp rice vinegar
- 1 tsp honey (or maple/agave syrup)
- juice of 1 lime
- ½ a small garlic clove, grated/crushed
- ½ tsp fine sea salt

Start with the vinagrete. Place a pan on high heat and once very hot, add the Scotch bonnet and cook, turning every now and then, until charred all over (3–5 minutes). Alternatively, use tongs to hold the chile and char it directly over an open flame.

Use a sharp knife to remove the top and bottom of the orange, then slice away the skin and outer pith. Cut between the pith to remove the segments, then chop into ¼ in (¾ cm) pieces. You want about 2 oz (60 g) of chopped flesh.

Place the orange flesh in a bowl and mix together with all the remaining ingredients for the vinagrete.

Deseed the charred chile, then finely chop it (don't peel, you want bits of charred skin). Add to the vinagrete a little at a time to get your desired heat level.

Melt the ghee in a small saucepan, then leave to cool for a few minutes (not long enough that it sets, you want it to be liquid and warm, but not piping hot).

Halve the scallops widthways and arrange on a platter. Sprinkle generously with sea salt flakes.

Spoon the melted ghee over the scallops, then follow with the vinagrete. Squeeze over plenty of fresh lime juice and serve.

Tropical shrimp with plantain and pickled shallots

This is easily one of my favorite recipes in the book. It's a bit of a labor of love, but I promise it's worth it.

To make it more manageable, you can marinate the shrimp, make the shrimp head oil and pickle the shallots up to a day in advance.

Inspired by one of my favorite *botecos* in Copacabana, Rio de Janeiro—Adega Pérola—a seafood bar that's been a local institution since 1956. This dish reimagines their Pérola Tropical—tropical pearl—which is a mix of shrimp and plantain marinated in garlic-infused oil. This version is much more elaborate, but the flavors are unmatched.

Serve straight away, as the plantain and shrimp will harden as they cool.

Serves 4 as an appetizer	GF
Prep time: 10–12 minutes	
Cook time: 17 minutes	

Shrimp and oil

12 × 1¼ oz (35 g) shell-on shrimp (15 oz/420 g total)
2 whole red bird's-eye chiles
2 whole green bird's-eye chiles
generous ½ cup (120 g) olive oil
fine sea salt
¾ tsp ground urucum (aka annatto/achiote, see page 23 for alternatives), plus a little to serve
3 tbsp tomato paste

Everything else

1 banana shallot, peeled and sliced into ⅛ in (3 mm) rings (use a mandoline if you have one)
¼ cup (60 g) lime juice (2–3 large limes)
1 tbsp rice vinegar
2 small, very ripe plantains
1 tbsp ghee (homemade or from a jar, not from a can)
2½ tsp ginger–garlic mix (page 26) or 2 small garlic cloves + ⅛ oz (5 g) fresh ginger, finely minced
2 tbsp cilantro stalks, very finely chopped

Remove the heads and peel the shells from the shrimp, keeping the tails on. Place the heads and shells in a frying pan off the heat. You should have about 9 oz (260 g) of peeled, tail-on shrimp.

Slice down the back of the shrimp to slightly butterfly them open, then devein them.

Place the peeled, tail-on shrimp in a bowl with the chiles, 1 tablespoon of the olive oil, ½ teaspoon of fine sea salt and the urucum. Gently mix and set aside.

To make the shrimp oil, add the tomato paste and a scant ½ cup (100 g) of olive oil to the pan of shrimp heads and shells. Place on high heat and stir-fry until the shells become bright pink, about 3½ minutes.

Place a sieve over a bowl and spoon the shrimp heads, shells and oil into the sieve. Press down on the heads to extract as much liquid and flavor as possible.

Put the sliced shallot into a separate bowl with the lime juice, vinegar and ½ teaspoon of fine sea salt. Mix and set aside.

Peel the plantains and cut into ¾ in (2 cm) thick rounds.

Wipe the frying pan clean. Add the ghee to the pan and place on very low heat. Once melted, add the plantain, spaced apart, and sprinkle over ¼ teaspoon of fine sea salt evenly. Cover with a lid and gently cook for 5 minutes, then flip the plantain and gently cook for another 5 minutes. You're not trying to brown or fry the plantain slices, you want them to steam and soften, so keep the heat low.

Pour the ghee into the bowl of shrimp oil and set the cooked plantain aside.

See page 160 for a recipe photo. →

Wipe the frying pan clean and place on high heat. Once very hot, add the shrimp and chiles to the pan, spread out as much as possible and fry for 1½ minutes on each side.

Remove the pan from the heat, then add the ginger–garlic mix, the shrimp head oil, the cooked plantain and the cilantro stalks.

Finely slice 1 of the red chiles and 1 of the green chiles, put them back into the pan and gently mix everything together.

Transfer to a platter and top with some of the pickled shallots (you won't need them all) and a sprinkling of urucum.

Drizzle over some of the shallot pickling liquid and serve with more fresh lime squeezed on top.

Coconut & cassava fried fish

I don't deep-fry food often, so trust me when I tell you this fried fish is worth it. Coated in a mixture of coconut and cassava, two of my favorite ingredients, it's crunchy and full of flavor thanks to the salty, tangy coconut marinade.

You can find *farinha de mandioca* (coarse dried cassava flour) in Brazilian speciality shops or in West African and Caribbean shops, under the name "garri" or "coarse cassava flour." Don't confuse it with cassava starch, which is a fine powder. If you can't get hold of it, polenta works well as a substitute.

Serves 4 as a snack — GF
Prep time: 5–10 minutes
Cook time: 6–8 minutes
Marinade time: 2 hours

- 14 oz (400 g) firm, skinless fish (such as sea bass, sea bream, tilapia)
- scant 1 cup (200 g) full-fat coconut milk (from a can, not carton; mix well before measuring)
- 2 tsp lime juice
- 1½ tsp fine sea salt
- 2½ cups (500 g) mild/light olive oil, for shallow-frying
- ⅛ oz (5 g) mix of cilantro and small basil leaves
- sea salt flakes
- 1 lime and 1 tangerine, to serve

Coating

- generous 1 cup (100 g) unsweetened shredded coconut
- ⅔ cup (100 g) coarse cassava flour (see note) or polenta
- ¼ cup (30 g) cornstarch
- ½ tsp medium curry powder, plus extra to serve
- ½ tsp fine sea salt
- plenty of freshly cracked pepper

Cut the fish into diagonal strips weighing around 1 oz (25 g) each.

Put the coconut milk, lime juice and salt into a medium container, mix well, then add the fish and gently stir to coat. Marinate for up to 2 hours at room temp, but preferably overnight, refrigerated (in which case remove from the fridge 1½ hours before frying).

Thoroughly mix all the coating ingredients together in a medium container.

A few strips at a time, remove the fish from the marinade—you want the strips to be covered in the coconut milk but not dripping—and place in the container of coating ingredients. Turn to thoroughly coat each piece, squeezing to help the coating adhere to the fish. Place the coated fillets on a tray and continue with the rest.

Line another tray or baking sheet with paper towels.

Put the oil into a medium pot and place on medium heat. Once the oil is hot (350°F/180°C, if you have a thermometer), carefully lower the fish pieces into the oil (it should sizzle if the oil is hot enough) and fry, turning every now and then, until crisp and golden brown all over (1½–2 minutes). Use a slotted spoon to transfer the fried fish to the lined tray or pan, then continue frying the rest.

Use the slotted spoon to remove all the bits from the oil. Very carefully add the herbs to the oil (stand back, as the oil may spit) and very quickly fry until crisp and bright green—this should only take about 10 seconds, so keep a close eye on it. Remove with a slotted spoon.

Transfer the fish to a platter and top with the crispy herbs. Finish with sea salt flakes and curry powder, squeeze over some fresh lime and tangerine juice and serve.

JORGE WASHINGTON

Jorge Washington is a larger-than-life character with a personality as iconic as his name. A chef and an actor, he's renowned in Salvador for his project *Culinária Musical* (musical cuisine), which celebrates Afro-Brazilian culture through food and music.

On the last Sunday of every month, Jorge (*zhor-zhee*) cooks up an Afro-Brazilian feast and invites Afro-Brazilian musicians and poets to perform as his guests eat. He carefully curates the line-up; the music starts off slow and mellow while you sit to eat and it gradually becomes louder and more energised until *everyone* is dancing and singing together. Jorge's parties draw a beautifully eclectic crowd. By combining his love of food and music, he's created a space for young, old and everyone in between to celebrate the intertwined Brazilian and African identity.

The setting for these parties—Casa do Benin, in Pelourinho, Salvador—is extremely significant. Salvador was the port into which most enslaved Africans were taken into Brazil and a center for Portuguese colonial power, and Pelourinho was once a site where enslaved people were punished. The cultural center Casa do Benin was established to preserve the connections between Brazil and West Africa, especially Benin, which was a key region in the transatlantic slave trade. The center is a physical symbol of resilience and pride that celebrates the ways in which African culture has enhanced Brazil.

Having been to a few of Jorge's parties over the years and struck up a friendship with him, I knew there was no better person to help showcase Afro-Bahian food in this book. A perfect example of Afro-Bahian fusion is the dish *maxixada*, which Jorge makes an exemplary version of (see photo on page 187). I asked him to take us on the journey of this dish he loves to cook so much, from its origin, to the market where he sources his ingredients, ending in Casa do Benin, where we cooked together.

Maxixada (*ma-shee-sha-da*) is a stew made with *maxixe* (*ma-shee-shee*), a spiky and slightly acidic cucumber variety, *dendê and* coconut milk (all native to West Africa), along with *carne de sol* (sun-dried beef) and dried shrimp. Walking through the Feira de São Joaquim with Jorge to source the ingredients was like being with a celebrity; everyone knew him and wanted to stop for a chat. Jorge confidently cut his way through the bustling market, making a beeline for his favorite stalls. He explained the importance of fostering relationships with vendors and growers, and that he went to different stalls for each of the ingredients, because he'd taken the time to work out who does what best. On the following page you can see the stall where he buys dried shrimp and the vendor he buys coconut from.

I'm incredibly grateful to Jorge for showing us his Salvador and for making the best *maxixada* I've ever tasted. Thank you also to my friend Nubya, who first introduced me to Jorge. If you're ever in Salvador on the last Sunday of the month, get yourself to one of Jorge's parties!

Main event pirão

Pirão (pee-rowng) is a dish which originated with the Indigenous Tupi Brazilians but was enhanced and embellished by enslaved people from Africa, who shaped Brazil's culinary identity, permeating the essence of Brazilian cooking with African soul. I first fell for *pirão* in Natal, in the north-east of Brazil, where my mother is from and where the beaches are peppered with fish shacks—humble restaurants in the sand, close enough to the sea that water laps up around your bare feet as the tide comes.

Pirão is a savory porridge made by beating coarse cassava flour (see page 20) into hot seafood stock, and it usually also contains scraps of fish or shrimp. It has a similar texture to wet polenta, and it's traditionally served as a side to *moqueca* (page 134). Those who have never tried *pirão* before often take a while to get used to the texture, which is soft and sort of sticky from the cassava starch. I adore the texture and have always thought the dish is special enough to take center stage, which is why I've created this main-event, celebratory version. The resulting dish is very similar to *bobó de camarão*; however, *bobó* contains coconut milk and is made with boiled, mashed cassava, rather than coarse cassava flour.

Serves 4 GF
Prep time: 10–15 minutes
Cook time: 34 minutes

- 12 large, shell-on shrimp
- 2 whole sea bream, scaled and gutted (see notes)
- 3 tbsp red palm oil (see page 20)
- 1 red Scotch bonnet chile (deseeded—you can leave this out if you prefer less heat)
- 3¾ cups (900 g) water
- fine sea salt
- ⅔ cup (100 g) coarse cassava flour (also called garri in West African and West Indian grocery stores) or quick-cook polenta
- olive oil
- 2 okra, thinly sliced into rounds
- 1 lime

Tomato chile paste

- 4 ripe vine tomatoes (12½ oz/360 g)
- 4 tbsp tomato paste
- 4 garlic cloves, peeled
- 1 small yellow onion, peeled and roughly chopped
- 2 large mild red chiles, roughly chopped
- 1¼ tsp sweet paprika
- 2 tbsp olive oil
- 1½ tsp fine sea salt

Peel the shrimp, putting the shells, heads and tails into a scraps bowl. Devein the shrimp, then chop each one into thirds and put into a separate bowl.

Fillet the sea bream, adding the heads and carcass to the scraps bowl of shrimp heads and shells. Remove and discard the skin from the fillets, roughly chop the flesh (size doesn't matter) and set aside in a separate bowl while you prepare the rest.

Put all the ingredients for the tomato chile paste into a blender or the small bowl of a food processor and blend to a paste. Add 3 tablespoons of the paste to the bowl of chopped shrimp, stir well, then set aside to marinate.

To make the stock, heat the red palm oil in a large, high-sided sauté pan on medium–high heat, then add the scraps (shrimp shells and heads, fish heads and carcass). Fry for 4 minutes, stirring until the shrimp shells become bright pink. Add the remaining tomato chile paste and the Scotch bonnet and stir-fry for 3 minutes, then add the water and ¼ teaspoon of fine sea salt and simmer gently for 15 minutes.

Meanwhile, put all the ingredients for the green chile vinagrete into a small bowl and set aside.

Allow the stock to cool for 5 minutes before straining through a sieve into a heatproof bowl, pushing down on the shrimp heads to extract all the liquid and flavor.

Return the strained stock to the sauté pan and add the chopped fish. Once simmering, start adding the cassava flour or polenta slowly, whisking vigorously as you go so there are no lumps. Don't worry about the fish breaking up, it's supposed to. Once all the flour has been added, turn the heat to the lowest and continue to whisk for another 6 minutes to get a wet polenta consistency. Set aside, covered.

recipe continues overleaf →

Seafood

Green chile vinagrete

1 green chile, very finely chopped
⅛ oz (5 g) cilantro, very finely chopped
2 tbsp olive oil
2 tbsp lime juice
⅛ tsp fine sea salt

Heat a medium frying pan on high heat with 1 tablespoon of olive oil. Add the shrimp and their marinade and fry for 1 minute on each side, until golden brown, then add 1 tablespoon of water, swirl and remove from the heat.

Top the pirão with the shrimp and some of the green chile vinagrete. Finish with the sliced okra, squeeze over some lime juice and serve.

Notes
Ask your fishmonger to fillet the sea bream if you like, keeping the heads and bones for the stock.

This is a long recipe, but it's well worth the effort and you can get ahead by making the stock and chile paste and marinating the shrimp a day ahead.

Seafood

Crab, coconut & zucchini omelet

I adore crab, as do most Brazilians! Crabs—*caranguejos*— are vital to Brazil's coastal ecosystems and culture, especially species like *caranguejo-uçá*, *guaiamum* and *siri*. They sustain mangroves, support marine life and star in dishes like *moqueca de siri* and, my favorite, *unha de caranguejo* (crab claw fritter—if you're ever in Rio, try them at the Belém Belém Amazônia restaurant in Copacabana). There's even a festival—the Festa do Caranguejo—which celebrates them as both a culinary delight and a coastal treasure. How wonderful!

The star of this omelet is, of course, the crab, which pairs beautifully with the coconut and zingy salsa. Any leftover salsa can be used as a condiment—with eggs, in sandwiches, on tacos, etc.

Serves 2 — GF
Prep time: 10 minutes
Cook time: 12–14 minutes

3 large eggs
scant 1 cup (200 g) full-fat coconut milk (from a can, not a carton; mix very well before measuring)
⅛ oz (5 g) scallion green ends, finely chopped (use the whites in another recipe)
⅛ oz (5 g) cilantro, finely chopped
⅛ oz (5 g) fresh chives, finely chopped, plus extra for serving
1 tsp lime zest
¾ tsp medium curry powder
1 small garlic clove, finely grated or crushed
fine sea salt
freshly cracked pepper
2 tbsp olive oil, plus extra to serve
1 large zucchini, roughly grated and squeezed to remove liquid
3½ oz (100 g) picked white crab meat
3 tbsp crème fraîche
sea salt flakes
1 lime, halved, to serve

Grated tomato salsa

2 ripe tomatoes (8 oz/230 g)
1 tbsp rice vinegar or lime juice
½ tbsp olive oil
1 small garlic clove, grated/crushed
1 tsp chopped chile condiment (page 29 or use hot sauce)
½ tsp sweet paprika (not smoked!)
½ tsp fine sea salt

For the salsa, halve the tomatoes, then deseed them. Grate into a bowl, using the large holes of a box grater—you should have 5 oz (140 g). Discard the tomato skins and stir in the rest of the ingredients.

Put the eggs, coconut milk, scallion green ends, herbs, lime zest, curry powder, garlic, ¼ teaspoon of fine sea salt and a good twist of pepper into a large bowl and whisk well.

Heat a nonstick frying pan on medium–high heat and add the 2 tablespoons of olive oil. Once hot, add the grated zucchini and ¼ teaspoon of fine sea salt and fry, stirring often, for about 6 minutes or until golden brown. Pour the egg mixture evenly over and cover with a lid. Cook for 6–8 minutes, or until set in the middle but still a little wet and soft on top (cook longer if you prefer).

Top the omelet with the crab. Strain the salsa so it's not soggy (keep the liquid for a Bloody Mary) and spoon over the omelet (you won't need it all).

Finish with crème fraîche, chopped chives and sea salt flakes, drizzle with olive oil and serve with the lime.

See page 172 for a recipe photo. →

Above Crab, coconut & zucchini omelet

Top Pastéis de forno with crunchy flaky spelt pastry
Bottom Cassava, shrimp & onion fritters

Coconut chicken with charred okra

Chicken and okra is a combination that can be found in many different cuisines—Indian, Chinese, West African, Creole, to name but a few. In Brazil, *frango com quiabo* (chicken with okra) is a typical dish from the state of Minas Gerais (see page 40), with roots in West African cooking (okra is native to West Africa and was brought to Brazil during the slave trade).

This version is inspired by (but very different to) the classic dish. Untraditionally, it features coconut milk in the sauce and coffee in the marinade, and rather than cooking the okra in the sauce (which makes it soft and slimy), I char it and serve it on top to preserve its crunch.

Serves 4 — GF
Prep time: 10 minutes
Cook time: 1 hour
Rest time: 10 minutes

8 chicken drumsticks
1 Scotch bonnet chile, whole (optional)

Sauce

1 tbsp olive oil
1 tsp Urfa pepper
1 tsp ground coffee
1 tsp fine sea salt
½ tsp smoked paprika
about 20 twists of freshly cracked pepper (⅛ tsp)

Marinade

1 × 14 oz (400 g) can of full-fat coconut milk
5¼ oz (150 g) sweet cherry tomatoes
1 red bell pepper, deseeded and quartered (6 oz/170 g)
3 small garlic cloves, peeled
⅛ oz (5 g) fresh ginger, peeled
1 Scotch bonnet chile, deseeded and finely chopped (or a milder chile if you prefer)
2 tbsp honey (or maple/agave syrup)
1 tbsp red palm oil (see page 20) or coconut oil
1½ tsp fine sea salt
1 tsp rice vinegar
½ tsp medium curry powder
¼ tsp smoked paprika
¼ tsp ground turmeric
about 50 twists of freshly cracked pepper (¼ tsp)

To serve

5 oz (140 g) okra, halved at an angle
olive oil
½ oz (15 g) picked cilantro leaves
½ oz (15 g) scallions, green ends thinly sliced
2 limes, halved
rice or flatbreads

Put the chicken and all the marinade ingredients into a large bowl and mix very well to coat the chicken evenly.

Put all the sauce ingredients into a blender and blend until smooth.

Heat a 10 in (26 cm) wide high-sided pot, for which you have a lid, on high heat. Once hot, add the chicken drumsticks, spaced apart as much as possible. Fry for about 8 minutes, turning every 2 minutes until browned all over.

Pour the sauce into the pot and mix so all the chicken drumsticks are coated. Add the whole Scotch bonnet (if using), cover with a lid and cook on high for 5 minutes. Lower the heat all the way down and cook for another 40 minutes, until the chicken is very soft. Leave to rest for 10 minutes. Squeeze the Scotch bonnet into the sauce to release its flavor (if using).

Meanwhile, heat a frying pan on high heat. Toss the okra with a little oil and fine salt, then add to the hot pan. Cook for about 6 minutes, turning a few times until charred all over. In a separate bowl, toss the charred okra with the cilantro and scallions.

Squeeze the juice of ½ a lime over the chicken, top with the okra and herbs and serve with rice or flatbreads and the rest of the limes.

Note
The marinade will make the pot a bit smoky, so make sure to open windows and turn on the extraction.

Lamb with pineapple pimenta & toasted cassava

This is inspired by *neua yang nam tok*—the Thai grilled steak salad with a hot, sour and sweet dressing. I'm using my pineapple pimenta (page 30) in the dressing and coarse cassava flour in the textural topping, instead of the traditional toasted rice. It's also great with pork shoulder steaks, marinated the same way and fried for 3 minutes on one side and 2 minutes on the other side.

You can find *farinha de mandioca* (coarse dried cassava flour) in Brazilian shops or in West African and Caribbean shops under the names "garri" or "coarse cassava flour." Don't confuse it with cassava starch, which is a fine powder. If you can't find it, polenta works well instead.

Serves 4	GF
Prep time: 10 minutes	
Cook time: 19 minutes	
Marinade/Rest time: 1 hour 15 minutes	

1 extra ripe pineapple (2 lb 10 oz/1.2 kg)
2 large yellow tomatoes (1 lb/500 g)
sea salt flakes
4 × 4½ oz (125 g) lamb neck fillets (1 lb/500 g)
⅛ oz (5 g) mint leaves
1 lime, halved, to serve

Marinade

1½ tbsp ghee (from a jar, not a can) or butter, softened
1 tbsp olive oil
2 tsp fine sea salt
1 tsp ground urucum (aka annatto/achiote, see page 23) or ¼ tsp sweet paprika and plenty of freshly cracked pepper
1 tsp Urfa or chipotle chile flakes

Pickled shallots

1 banana shallot, thinly sliced into rounds
3 tbsp lime juice (2 small limes)
½ tsp fine sea salt

Toasted cassava

2 tbsp coarse dried cassava flour (see intro) or polenta
1 tbsp black sesame seeds
1 tsp sea salt flakes
½ tsp medium curry powder

Dressing

¼ cup (60 g) pineapple pimenta (page 30)
1½ tbsp lime juice
1 tbsp honey (or maple/agave syrup)
2 tsp rice vinegar

Peel and core the pineapple. Halve lengthways, then use half to make the pineapple pimenta (page 30) or skip to the next step if you have some already made.

Cut the other half of the pineapple into ⅛ in (4 mm) thick slices. Slice the tomatoes into ⅛ in (4 mm) thick rounds. Arrange on a platter, sprinkle with sea salt flakes and set aside.

Mix all the marinade ingredients together in a bowl, add the lamb and mix to thoroughly coat the lamb. Set aside to marinate for 1 hour at room temperature.

Put all the pickled shallot ingredients into a small bowl and mix. Set aside.

Preheat the oven to 375°F (190°C). Prepare a baking pan to finish the lamb in the oven.

Put all the toasted cassava ingredients into a medium frying pan and place on high heat. Cook for about 5 minutes, tossing the pan until the cassava is golden brown and toasted. Transfer to a bowl and put the pan back on high heat.

Make sure the pan is very hot, then add the lamb, spaced apart. Fry for 3 minutes or until nicely browned. Flip and cook for another 3 minutes on the other side, or until browned. Flip to cook on the last two sides for about 1 minute each, or until browned.

Transfer to the prepared baking pan and roast in the oven for 3 minutes, then flip the fillets and cook for another 3 minutes. Remove from the oven, transfer the lamb to a board or plate and set aside to rest for 15 minutes.

Meanwhile, mix all the dressing ingredients together.

Slice the lamb into ¼ in (¾ cm) thick slices and season generously with sea salt flakes. Arrange on top of the sliced tomatoes and pineapple, then spoon over plenty of the dressing.

Finish with the pickled shallots, mint leaves and some of the toasted cassava and sesame mixture, crushing it between your fingertips. Squeeze over some fresh lime juice and serve.

MIDDLE EASTERN IMMIGRATION

Brazil is home to many diverse Middle Eastern communities, the three largest being Lebanese, Syrian and Palestinian. Immigration first started at the end of the nineteenth century, after the fall of the Ottoman Empire and the socio-political and economic instability that ensued.

The first major wave of immigration occurred between 1890 and 1920, as many Lebanese and Syrians fled economic hardship, famine and the upheaval that followed the empire's collapse. A second wave followed after World War II, driven by the establishment of Israel and the resulting displacement of Palestinians. Immigration continued throughout the mid-20th century and waves of Middle Eastern migration have continued into the 21st century, particularly from Syria since the onset of the Syrian Civil War in the 2010s. These waves have been fueled by political unrest, violence and the search for better economic opportunities. Given the Israeli military assaults on Gaza and Lebanon, it's likely that immigration from these regions will increase, especially since Brazil's president, Luiz Inácio Lula da Silva, has been a strong advocate for Palestinian rights and for welcoming refugees.

As of 2024, Brazil has the largest Lebanese diaspora in the world. An estimated 7–10 million Brazilians are of full or partial Lebanese descent, which, incidentally, is much more than the population of Lebanon itself. There are approximately 3–4 million people of Syrian descent in Brazil and around 100,000 people of Palestinian descent.

All this to say that Levantine cuisine has had a *huge* impact on Brazil, so much so that Middle Eastern restaurants are ubiquitous in Brazil and you can find *kibe* (ground meat and bulgur fritters) and *esfiha* (open-faced meat pies) on the counters of pretty much every café and juice bar across the country. (*Kibe* and *esfiha* are the Brazilian spellings of *kibbeh* and *'sfiha*, which of course are also an anglicization of the Arabic.)

As a child visiting Brazil, one of my favorite places to eat was Habib's—a Brazilian Lebanese fast-food chain with an outlet in the shopping center in my mom's home town of Natal. Growing up, I didn't question the origin of the *kibe* and *esfiha* I loved so much and it didn't occur to me they might not be Brazilian; I just knew that I loved them.

When I first started working in the Ottolenghi Test Kitchen in 2016, I knew a lot about Italian, Brazilian and Mexican food because those were the cuisines I grew up with, but I knew very little about Middle Eastern cuisine. One day, Sami Tamimi was in the Test Kitchen making *'sfiha* and I remember thinking to myself how cool it was that he was making a Brazilian dish. Of course he was not, and what I didn't know at the time was that *'sfiha* was in fact a Levantine dish with Palestinian, Lebanese and Syrian iterations.

Now I'm older, a little wiser and aware of the origins of my favorite childhood dishes. I love the crossover between Middle Eastern and Brazilian culture and cuisine, see my take on charutos Libanais on the next page.

Charutos with spicy tomato broth & garlic oil

Lebanese food is my go-to when I'm in Brazil and I need a break from Brazilian food. My favorite Lebanese restaurant in Rio de Janeiro—Basha—makes the most incredible meat-stuffed cabbage rolls, *charutos Libanais* (which literally means Lebanese cigars and is the Portuguese name for the dish *malfouf*). They come swimming in a fragrant tomato broth and are served with *pimenta caseira* (homemade hot sauce) and a plate of lime to squeeze over, in a beautiful union of Lebanese and Brazilian cuisine. The following recipe is inspired by this dish.

Makes 12 rolls — GF
Prep time: 20 minutes
Cook time: 9 minutes

9 oz (250 g) rainbow chard or Swiss chard
1 tbsp olive oil
1 Scotch bonnet chile
2 limes, halved

Filling

14 oz (400 g) ground lamb
3 tbsp tomato paste
½ oz (15 g) cilantro, finely chopped
½ a yellow onion, peeled and grated (2 oz/60 g)
1 garlic clove, finely grated/crushed
½ tsp medium curry powder
½ tsp dried mint
¼ tsp ground allspice
1 tsp fine sea salt
about 50 twists of freshly cracked pepper (¼ tsp)

Broth

1 tbsp tomato paste
¼ tsp fine sea salt

Garlic oil

1½ tbsp olive oil
1½ tbsp salted butter
3 garlic cloves, very finely chopped
¼ tsp Urfa pepper flakes
⅛ tsp fine sea salt

Put all the filling ingredients into a bowl, mix well and set aside.

Fill your kettle to its max and boil. For the broth, whisk 7 oz (200 g) of boiling water with the tomato paste and salt in a medium bowl. Set aside.

To blanch the leaves, hold the bunch of chard by the stalk over a large pan (see photo overleaf). Pour the rest of the boiling water from the kettle all over the leaves, to soften them and make them easier to roll.

Cut the stalks off the leaves (check the photo overleaf to see how much stalk to cut off). Chop 3½ oz (100 g) of the stalks as finely as possible and mix with the lamb filling. Use the rest of the stalks in another recipe.

Clean your surface and lightly grease with olive oil. Lay the leaves flat, rib side up, taking care not to rip them. If the leaves are larger you'll need just one per roll; if they're smaller you may need to use two or three overlapping each other—as per the photo overleaf.

Fill each leaf with about 1¾ oz (50 g) of the lamb filling, then fold in the sides and roll them up tightly. You should make about 12 rolls. Place on a pan, seam-side down.

Place a 11 in (28 cm) wide pan, for which you have a lid, on high heat. Add 1 tablespoon of olive oil and once hot, place the chard rolls in the pan, seam side down. Fry for 2½ minutes on each side, so both sides are nicely browned. Pour over the tomato broth and add the whole Scotch bonnet. Turn down the heat to low, cover with a lid and cook for 4 minutes.

Meanwhile, put all the garlic oil ingredients into a small saucepan on medium heat. Gently cook for 3 minutes, or until the garlic is soft, golden brown and fragrant (take care not to burn the garlic!).

Squeeze the Scotch bonnet into the sauce to release its flavor. Drizzle the rolls with some of the garlic oil, serving the rest on the side. Squeeze over plenty of fresh lime juice, and serve.

Chicken in beet sauce

One of my mom's favorite dishes is *frango ao molho pardo* (chicken in brown sauce), a dish typical of the state of Rio Grande do Norte, where my mom's family is from, as well as in the state of Minas Gerais. The dish is made with deeply caramelized onions and—crucially—fresh chicken blood, both of which contribute to the resulting rich, brown sauce.

In theory, I am very much of the belief that if you're going to eat animals, you should be able to eat all of the animal—and thus the idea of cooking with blood shouldn't be off-putting. In practice, however, I am nothing but a hypocrite and thus I wanted to create a version of this dish without the blood. Enter . . . beet juice, which is similar in color, with comparable sweet and iron-ey undertones. The resulting sauce is deliciously rich and slightly sweet from the caramelized onions and beet juice—reminiscent of a reduced red wine sauce. My mom says it's *"melhor que o original"*—better than the original. Hopefully that's enough encouragement for you to make it!

You'll make more *tempero verde* than you need. Keep it refrigerated for up to 2 weeks and use it as a marinade for veggies, seafood and meats, as a condiment or a salsa, or stirred into soups and stews.

Serves 4 GF
Prep time: 5–10 minutes
Marinade time: 20 minutes
Cook time: 1 hour and 13–20 minutes

Marinade (tempero verde)
½ cup (100 g) olive oil
1¾ oz (50 g) scallions (about 3), roughly chopped
1 oz (25 g) cilantro
1 oz (25 g) fresh parsley
½ oz (15 g) garlic (about 5)
⅓ oz (10 g) fresh ginger, peeled
1 mild green chile, stalk removed
1 tsp fine sea salt

Chicken
4 skin-on chicken drumsticks
4 skin-on, bone-in chicken thighs
1 tbsp rice vinegar
fine sea salt
olive oil
2 yellow onions, peeled and finely chopped (8 oz/220 g)
2 plum tomatoes, finely chopped (8 oz/220 g)
¾ tsp ground ginger
¾ tsp ground cumin
freshly cracked pepper
2 cups (500 g) beet juice
2 lemons, halved

Put all the ingredients for the marinade into a food processor and pulse to get a finely chopped paste.

Put the chicken into a large bowl with about ¼ cup (60 g) of the marinade, the rice vinegar and 1 teaspoon of fine sea salt. Mix well and leave to marinate for 20 minutes.

Place a 12 in (30 cm) Dutch oven (for which you have a lid) on medium-high heat and brush with a little oil. Once hot, add the chicken and fry for 8–10 minutes, turning halfway until browned on both sides. Don't worry if the bottom starts to catch and burn—this is creating flavor and depth that you'll scrape into the sauce later. Transfer the chicken to a plate.

Without cleaning the pot, add 1 tablespoon of olive oil, the onions, tomatoes, spices, ¾ teaspoon of fine sea salt and plenty of freshly cracked black pepper (about 100 twists of the grinder/½ teaspoon). Fry, stirring, until soft and deeply browned, 8–10 minutes. Again, don't worry that the mixture is catching.

Pour over the beet juice and use a wooden spoon to get all that flavor off the bottom of the pot and into the sauce. Return the chicken to the pot, skin side down, then cover with a lid. Turn the heat all the way down and cook for 45 minutes.

Remove the lid and turn the chicken skin side up. Increase the heat to medium and continue to cook, uncovered, for 12–15 minutes, stirring every now and then, until the sauce has thickened and reduced to the consistency in the picture.

Leave to rest for 5 minutes, then skim away any excess fat. Mix 2 tablespoons of the marinade with the juice of a lemon and serve with the chicken, along with more lemon wedges.

Note
You can use a whole chicken chopped into parts instead of the legs and thighs, if you prefer, in which case use the carcass to make a stock for another recipe (e.g. page 96).

Mango and urucum chicken

I love the combination of meat and fruit, and in this recipe, *urucum* (oo-roo-koom) brings subtle peppery notes that pair beautifully with the chicken and mango. It also adds a vibrant orange-red color to the oil. *Urucum* is a red seed from the *urucuzeiro* tree, also known as achiote in Mexico and Central America, and annatto in the Caribbean and English-speaking countries. Indigenous peoples in Brazil have used *urucum* for centuries as body paint for rituals, as a natural sunscreen, and as a symbol of life and protection.

For this recipe and others throughout the book, I grind the seeds down to a powder in a spice grinder. You can find *urucum* in seed, powder, or paste form in Latin American food stores (labeled as achiote), Caribbean food stores (usually called annatto), or online. If you can't get it, use sweet (not smoked) paprika and black pepper instead.

Avoid juice with added sugar or flavorings. If you can't get pure mango juice, use pineapple juice or pure juice mixes, like mango and apple or mango and orange.

Serves 4 — GF
Prep time: 5–10 minutes
Cook time: 1 hour
Marinade time: 1 hour
Rest time: 10 minutes

6 chicken legs
scant 1 cup (200 g) pure mango juice (see intro)
1 extra-ripe Alphonso mango, chopped into 1 in (3 cm) pieces (5¼ oz/150 g)
1 small yellow onion, peeled, cut into eighths, and layers separated
4 garlic cloves, peeled and crushed with the side of a knife
4 allspice berries, roughly crushed
1 cinnamon stick, broken
1½ tbsp rice vinegar
½ tsp sweet paprika (not smoked!)

Marinade

¼ cup (60 g) yogurt
2 tsp ground urucum (or ½ tsp sweet paprika plus 30 twists of cracked black pepper)
2 tsp chopped red chile condiment (page 29, or use store-bought)
2 tsp fine sea salt

To serve

1 lime, halved
1 tangerine, halved

Mix all the marinade ingredients together in a large bowl. Add the chicken and mix to coat thoroughly. Leave to marinate for at least 1 hour at room temperature (or overnight, refrigerated, in which case bring back to room temp 2 hours before cooking).

Preheat the oven to 475°F (240°C).

Put the mango juice, mango pieces, onion, garlic, allspice, cinnamon, vinegar and sweet paprika into a 9 × 14 in (23 × 36 cm) roasting pan and stir together. Arrange the chicken legs on top, skin side up and spaced apart.

Roast for 25 minutes, then turn the heat down to 350°F (180°C) and roast for another 35 minutes (no need to baste). Remove from the oven and rest for 10 minutes.

Transfer the chicken and sauce to a platter. Squeeze over plenty of lime and tangerine juice and serve.

CASSAVA AND TUCUPI

In Brazil, the root most commonly known around the world as cassava or manioc goes by different names—*aipim, macaxeira, mandioca*—depending on where you're from and what you're referring to. *Macaxeira* (from the Tupi-Guarani "*maka'xeira*") is the word predominantly used in the north-east of Brazil where my mother is from, so that's how I've always known it.

There are two types of manioc. The white-fleshed variety is ubiquitous in Brazilian cuisine, beloved by all, and has countless uses. The whole root can be peeled and boiled, then fried or mashed, or it can be processed into products like *tapioca* (a fine flour made from the starch) and *farinha de mandioca* (toasted coarse cassava flour). Then there's the wild yellow variety, from which communities in the Brazilian Amazon make a sacred ingredient called *tucupi*.

Tucupi is a bright yellow liquid extracted from wild manioc, which is toxic in its raw form due to high levels of cyanuric acid. To make it safe for consumption, it needs to be boiled and fermented. This wondrous ingredient has been crafted by Indigenous communities of the Brazilian Amazon for thousands of years and showcases their remarkable ingenuity.

I love the flavor of *tucupi*, which is sour, savory, funky, completely delicious and utterly addictive. When I first tasted it in the form of *pimenta no tucupi,* a hot sauce made with *tucupi*, I became so obsessed that I ended up adding it to everything—and even drinking it straight from the bowl. I got quite sick and learned the hard way that if you're not used to *tucupi*, it has to be consumed in moderation. Otherwise, you might experience extreme stomach cramps and other unpleasant effects I won't describe here!

There's no single way to make *tucupi*; each community has its own way of making it and these traditions are passed down from generation to generation. I've seen *tucupi* being made in two different ways. In 2023 we visited the Comunidade Ribeirinha Santo Antônio, a *caboclo* (a person of mixed Indigenous and European descent) community in the Anavilhanas Archipelago, and here they made it following traditional Indigenous methods using no machinery. The matriarch of the community, Dona Rosa (who described herself as "*a filha da floresta"*—the daughter of the forest), demonstrated the process.

First she peeled and grated the toxic wild yellow *mandioca,* then she passed it through a woven *tipití* to extract the liquid (if you ever played with those woven

Meat

finger traps as a child, it kind of looks like a very big version of that). The extracted liquid was then left to rest for about six hours, during which time the starch separated from the liquid. After that, the liquid fermented for a few days (the longer it ferments the more acidic, lively and bubbly it becomes, she explained), and then it was boiled to cook off the cyanuric acid.

Tucupi is used to make traditional dishes like *pato no tucupi* (duck cooked in *tucupi* with *jambú*—an Amazonian mouth-numbing plant—see my version on page 200), *tacacá* (a dried shrimp soup made with *goma de mandioca,* a jelly made from *mandioca* starch), *pimenta no tucupi* (a chile and tucupi hot sauce) and *arroz de pato no tucupi* (duck rice cooked with tucupi, see my version on page 217).

In 2024, Romã's family friend Antônio took us to visit his mother Antônia and her partner Cloltido, who make *tucupi* and *farinha* in a process that involves some motorised machinery in their beautiful home a few hours down the Amazon river from *Manaus*. On the opposite page, you can see this process, which is similar to the above description but uses a machine fed by a booted worker to turn the soaked manioc into pulp. During this process, nothing is wasted. The peelings are fed to their cows (see page 198), chickens and pigs, the coarse flour is used to make *farinha*, the starch is dried and used as a thickener and the squeezed pulp is used to make flatbreads and cakes.

Since *tucupi* is almost impossible to source outside the Amazon region, I've created a recipe on page 200 to replicate its unique sour, salty, funky flavor, using a combination of yellow tomatoes, ginger, onion, lime and salt.

Duck in golden tomato broth

This dish is inspired by the traditional Amazonian dish *pato no tucupi* (duck in tucupi) (more on page 197). *Tucupi* is impossible to come by outside of Brazil, but I'm completely obsessed with it, so I was determined to come up with something that tastes similar, using easily accessible ingredients. I've always thought that *tucupi* tastes like fermented yellow tomatoes and so this formed the basis of the broth in my version, along with lime, onion, ginger and garlic. The watercress is reminiscent of *jambú* leaves in the classic recipe—an Amazonian leafy herb, the flowering seeds of which have a very similar flavor and tingling/numbing sensation to Sichuan pepper.

Serves 4 — GF
Prep time: 10 minutes
Cook time: 2 hours 15 minutes

6 duck legs
fine sea salt
freshly cracked pepper
5½ oz (160 g) watercress
2 limes, halved, to serve

Broth

1 lb (500 g) orange cherry tomatoes (e.g. Sungold)
2 cups (500 g) water
½ a yellow onion (2 oz/60 g), peeled
½ oz (15 g) fresh ginger, peeled
1 garlic clove, peeled
1 tsp rice vinegar
1¼ tsp fine sea salt
½ deseeded Scotch bonnet or 1 bird's-eye chile (or more/less to taste)
a small pinch of saffron threads
about 20 twists of freshly cracked pepper (⅛ tsp)

Using the sharp point of a knife or skewer, poke the skin of the duck legs all over, including underneath and especially any particularly fatty parts. Place in a high-sided roasting pan and season with 1½ teaspoons of fine sea salt and plenty of pepper (about 50 twists of the grinder/¼ teaspoon). Mix to coat the legs thoroughly and evenly, then arrange skin side up.

Transfer to a non-preheated oven. Turn the heat up to 325°F (170°C) and roast for 2 hours, or until the skin is crisp and well browned and the meat is very soft.

Meanwhile, make the broth. Put all the ingredients into a blender and blend until smooth. Place a sieve over an 11 in (28 cm) wide pot/Dutch oven off the heat. Strain the liquid through the sieve into the pot, pushing down on the pulp to extract as much liquid as possible. Discard the pulp.

Once the duck has finished roasting, bring the broth to a simmer over medium heat. Once simmering, lower the heat, add the duck legs and very gently cook for 10 minutes, or until the meat softens.

Stir in the watercress and, once it's wilted, remove from the heat. Finish with a good squeeze of fresh lime juice and some chopped chile.

Notes
Try to get ripe orange cherry tomatoes, e.g. Sungold, as these will help to create a bright yellow broth. The broth is delicious and extremely versatile.

For a quicker meal, bring to a simmer and add marinated fish, shrimp, tofu or thinly sliced meat to quickly poach in the liquid.

Slow-cooked pineapple pork with green vinagrete

This dish is intentionally as hands off as possible—there's no marinating or searing of meat involved, everything just goes into the pot at the same time and a few hours later you have delicious fall-apart meat that's spiced from the cinnamon and Scotch bonnet and sweet from the pineapple.

Try to get a piece of pork with plenty of intramuscular fat.

Serve with rice, flatbreads or soft corn tortillas.

Serves 4 — GF
Prep time: 10 minutes
Cook time: 2 hours 50 minutes
Rest time: 15 minutes

- 1 lb 3 oz (1 kg) pork collar or shoulder
- 6½ oz (180 g) soft, extra ripe pineapple, cut into 1½ in (4 cm) pieces
- 1 lime, halved

Sauce

- 4¼ cups (1 liter) pineapple juice
- 1 medium yellow onion, peeled, halved and thinly sliced (4 oz/120 g)
- 4 garlic cloves, peeled
- 2 cinnamon sticks
- 1 Scotch bonnet chile
- ½ tsp sweet paprika
- 1 tbsp ground urucum (aka annatto/achiote, see page 23) or add another ½ tsp sweet paprika
- 1 tsp smoked chile flakes (such as Urfa, chipotle or ancho)
- 1 tbsp rice vinegar
- ½ tbsp fine sea salt
- ½ tbsp mixed peppercorns, crushed

Vinagrete

- ½ oz (15 g) cilantro
- ½ a yellow onion, peeled
- 1 green chile
- 4 tbsp olive oil
- 2 tsp rice vinegar
- ¼ tsp fine sea salt

Preheat the oven to 325°F (170°C).

Remove the skin from the pork and cut it into 2¾ in (7 cm) chunks. Put the pork and all the ingredients for the sauce into a 12 in (30 cm) Dutch oven or ovensafe pot with a lid. Mix well, then cover the pork with a circle of parchment paper and place the lid on the pot. Transfer to the oven for 2½ hours.

After 2½ hours, increase the oven temperature to 410°F (210°C). Remove the pot from the oven and take off the lid and paper. Add the pineapple pieces, stir gently and return to the oven for 20 minutes, uncovered, until the meat has browned on top and the fruit has softened. Remove the Scotch bonnet (squeeze it first to release its flavor into the sauce). Stir the pork together with the sauce and leave to rest for 15 minutes.

For the vinagrete, very finely chop the cilantro, onion and green chile and mix with the oil, vinegar and salt.

Squeeze the juice of a lime over the pork, spoon over the vinagrete and serve.

Vaca atolada

Vaca atolada—cow stuck in the mud—is a stew of beef ribs and *macaxeira* (page 21), typical of Minas Gerais. It's also the name of one of my favorite bars in Rio de Janeiro, a left-wing hangout frequented by *Lulistas* (supporters of President Lula), with live samba every night. If you're in Rio, I highly recommend going.

As well as thickening the sauce, *macaxeira*/cassava lends a natural sweetness to the dish. If you can't find cassava, use peeled pumpkin or squash instead, cut into larger 3 in (8 cm) chunks so they don't cook too quickly and become mushy in the stew. Watercress or thinly sliced greens are another great addition—add them at the end along with the cilantro, to quickly cook in the residual heat.

Serves 4 — GF
Prep time: 15 minutes
Cook time: 2 hours 46–52 minutes
Rest time: 20 minutes

- 4 × 9 oz (250 g) beef short ribs (1 lb 3 oz/1 kg total)
- 2 tbsp olive oil
- ½ tbsp fine sea salt
- freshly cracked pepper
- 1 lb 3 oz (1 kg) cassava
- 2 yellow onions, peeled and thinly sliced
- 3½ cups (800 g) water
- 1 Scotch bonnet
- ⅓ oz (10 g) cilantro, plus extra to serve
- 1 lime, halved

Sauce

- 2–3 vine tomatoes, roughly chopped (10 oz/280 g)
- 1½ tbsp tomato paste
- 100 twists of freshly cracked pepper (½ tsp)
- 3 tbsp ginger–garlic mix (page 26) or ⅓ oz (10 g) each garlic and ginger, peeled and finely chopped
- 2 tbsp rice vinegar
- 2 tbsp Worcestershire sauce
- 2 cinnamon sticks
- 1 tbsp honey (or maple/agave syrup)
- ½ tbsp ground urucum (annatto/achiote, page 23)
- ½ tbsp fine sea salt
- 1 tsp ground cumin

Grated tomatoes

- 2 ripe tomatoes (8 oz/230 g)
- 1 tbsp rice vinegar or lime juice
- ½ tbsp olive oil
- 1 small garlic clove, grated/crushed
- 1 tsp chopped red chile condiment (page 29) or hot sauce
- ½ tsp sweet paprika (not smoked!)
- ½ tsp fine sea salt

Put the short ribs into a bowl with 1 tablespoon of the olive oil, ½ tablespoon of fine sea salt and plenty of pepper. Mix well and set aside.

Prepare the cassava. Peel away the thick brown skin and the pinkish layer beneath it and remove any soft or blackened parts. Cut the cassava into 2½ in (6 cm) long cylinders, then halve each piece lengthways. Remove the hard fiber running through the center, either by pulling it out or cutting it away with a knife. Place in a bowl of water as you go to stop it browning and set aside.

Put all the sauce ingredients into a bowl, mix and set aside.

Place a 12 in (30 cm) Dutch oven or heavy-bottomed pot for which you have a lid on high heat. Once very hot, add the ribs to the pot, spaced apart. Sear the ribs to get a good, dark brown crust on each side, 1–3 minutes per side. Remove the ribs and set aside on a plate.

Lower the heat to medium and remove the fat, leaving about 1 tablespoon in the pot (if you don't have enough, use 1 tablespoon of olive oil). Add the onions and fry, stirring often, until they are soft and well browned, 8–10 minutes. Scrape up all of the dark crust at the bottom of the pot as you cook—this adds flavor.

Once the onions are well browned, add the sauce ingredients and cook, stirring often, for about 6 minutes, or until thickened and jammy. Remove the cassava from the water and add to the pot along with the ribs. Stir well so everything is coated in the red mixture.

Pour over the water (the ribs won't be completely covered but this is enough liquid) and add the Scotch bonnet. Cover the surface of the liquid with a circle of parchment paper, then place the lid on the pot. Turn the heat all the way down to low and cook for 2½ hours, or until the meat is very soft. Turn off the heat and leave to rest, covered, for 20 minutes.

Meanwhile prepare the grated tomatoes. Halve the tomatoes, then deseed them. Grate into a bowl, using the large holes of a box grater—you should have 5 oz (140 g). Discard the skins and stir in all the remaining ingredients.

Skim any excess fat from the surface of the stew, then stir in the cilantro sprigs and lime juice. Serve with the grated tomatoes spooned on top, and more cilantro.

Chicken, bacon & scallion skewers with stroganoff sauce

You might be wondering why a stroganoff recipe features in a book about Brazil, but over 2 million Brazilians have Russian or Eastern European roots and as a result, *estrogonofe* (pronounced *es-tro-go-no-fee*) has become one of Brazil's most beloved dishes. In fact, I would go so far as to say that most Brazilians probably think this is a local dish, or at least don't question its origin. It's truly a staple in restaurants and homes across the country.

Typically made with beef or chicken and served with rice and *batata palha* (crispy, fried potato sticks), Brazilian *estrogonofe* features ketchup and cream and is milder than the original style. While inspired by stroganoff, my version unapologetically diverges from both the eastern European and Brazilian versions.

Serves 4 — GF
Prep time: 10–15 minutes
Cook time: 30 minutes

Skewers

- 4 × 12 in (30 cm) metal skewers (or wooden skewers soaked in water)
- 4 skin-on, boneless chicken thighs, quartered
- 2 tbsp olive oil
- ½ tsp rice vinegar
- ¾ tsp fine sea salt
- 30 twists of freshly cracked pepper (⅛ tsp)
- 1 bunch of scallions, cut into 2 in (5 cm) lengths (3½ oz/100 g)
- 3½ oz (100 g) bacon strips, cut in half

Sauce

- ¾ cup (180 g) water
- 4 tsp English mustard
- 2 garlic cloves, roughly chopped
- 1 tbsp rice vinegar
- ½ tsp sweet paprika
- ½ tsp tomato paste
- 50 twists of freshly cracked pepper (¼ tsp)
- ⅛ tsp fine sea salt

To serve

- ⅓ cup (80 g) Greek yogurt or sour cream (I use sheep's yogurt)
- batata palha (page 31; see note)
- ½ oz (15 g) scallion green ends, julienned
- 2 green chiles, thinly sliced into rounds
- 1 lime, halved

Put the chicken, oil, vinegar, salt and pepper into a large bowl and mix well.

Rinse the scallion pieces; you want them to be wet to ensure they don't burn in the oven.

Preheat the oven to 425°F (220°C).

Add all the sauce ingredients to a 10 × 12½ in (25 × 32 cm) high-sided roasting pan and whisk to combine. Place a rack on top of the pan.

Thread the skewers. Start with a piece of scallion, then a piece of chicken with the skin side facing up, then a folded piece of bacon. Repeat to fill the skewers, then arrange them on the rack, skin side up.

Transfer (the pan and rack) to the oven and bake for 10 minutes. Lower the heat to 400°F (200°C) and continue to bake for 20 minutes. Remove from the oven and lift the skewers onto a chopping board. Use a blowtorch to give the chicken a little more color.

Add the yogurt to the pan of sauce and whisk until smooth.

Top the skewers with the scallions, green chiles and the batata palha (optional). Squeeze over some lime juice and serve with the sauce alongside.

Note

I serve these with *batata palha* (page 31) but it's very much an optional topping as frying can be a bit of a chore. If you're up for the challenge, start by making the *batata palha* to get all the frying out the way.

Green pancakes with yogurt sauce

Panquecas com molho branco (pancakes with white sauce), inspired by the Italian dish *crespelle*, is a very popular Brazilian–Italian dish in which savory pancakes are filled with ground meat or chicken, rolled up and then covered with a white sauce. It was my *bisavó* (great-grandmother) Eugênia's favorite dish.

My untraditional version features green pancakes, a yogurt sauce and a zingy salsa to cut through the richness, making it much lighter and brighter than the original. The recipe may seem a little long, but all the elements are very straightforward. Get ahead by making the ground beef, yogurt sauce and grated tomatoes up to a day in advance, then all you have to do is make the pancakes, fill them and bake.

Another great version of this dish, if you don't want to make pancakes, is to stuff the meat inside grilled romano peppers. To do this, turn the oven to the highest broiler setting. Place the peppers on a pan and broil for 7 minutes. Cut a slit in each pepper, deseed and pat the insides dry, then fill with the cooked meat, cover with the yogurt sauce and bake.

Serves 4 — GF
Prep time: 15 minutes
Cook time: 42–44 minutes

1 lb (500 g) ground beef
1½ oz (40 g) Parmesan, grated, to serve
⅛ oz (5 g) fresh basil, thinly sliced

Umami paste for ragù

1 yellow onion, peeled and roughly chopped
4 garlic cloves, peeled
2 red chiles, deseeded and roughly chopped
⅓ cup (80 g) tomato paste
⅓ cup (60 g) olive oil
½ oz (15 g) dried mixed/wild mushrooms
1¼ tsp fine sea salt
¾ tsp ground cumin
½ tsp fennel seeds
⅛ tsp ground cinnamon
about 80 twists of freshly cracked pepper (about ½ tsp)

Pancakes

1⅓ cups (300 g) milk (regular or plant-based)
5¼ oz (150 g) baby spinach
1½ cups (150 g) spelt flour (or all-purpose flour)
3 eggs
olive oil, for frying

Preheat the oven to 475°F (240°C).

Put all the ingredients for the paste into a blender and blend until smooth, scraping down the sides as needed. Transfer the paste to a 12 in (30 cm) ovenproof cast-iron pan or baking dish. Don't clean the blender—you'll use it again for the pancake batter.

Add the ground beef to the dish of paste. Mix very well to combine, then bake for 12 minutes. Remove from the oven and set aside.

While the meat mixture is cooking, put all the pancake ingredients into the blender and blend until completely smooth. Heat a frying pan on medium–high heat and brush with a little olive oil. Once the pan is very hot, pour in some of the batter and swirl to get a pancake about 8 in (20 cm) wide. Cook for 2 minutes, then flip and cook for another 30 seconds. Continue with the rest of the batter, to make 8 pancakes.

Transfer the meat mixture to a bowl. You'll use the ovenproof pan/dish again, so there's no need to clean it.

Fill each pancake with ⅛ of the meat mixture, roll up and arrange seam side down in the ovenproof pan.

recipe continues overleaf →

Yogurt sauce

scant 1 cup (200 g) Greek yogurt
2 tbsp cornstarch
2 egg yolks
2 tbsp boiling water
½ a small garlic clove, crushed/finely grated
¼ tsp fine sea salt
plenty of nutmeg, finely grated (or a pinch of ground nutmeg)

Grated tomatoes

2 ripe tomatoes (8 oz/230 g)
1 tbsp rice vinegar or lime juice
½ tbsp olive oil
1 small garlic clove, grated/crushed
1 tsp chopped red chile condiment (page 29) or hot sauce
½ tsp sweet paprika (not smoked!)
½ tsp fine sea salt

Whisk all the ingredients for the yogurt sauce together until completely smooth, then spoon over the pancakes. Drizzle evenly with oil, then bake for 10–12 minutes, or until lightly browned on top. Finish under the broiler for a few minutes to get extra color.

Meanwhile make the grated tomatoes. Halve the tomatoes, then deseed them. Grate into a bowl using the large holes of a box grater—you should have 5 oz (140 g). Discard the tomato skins and stir in all the remaining ingredients.

Spoon the grated tomatoes over the pancakes (you may want to strain them a little first). Drizzle with olive oil and finish with grated Parmesan, basil and plenty of pepper.

JAPANESE IMMIGRATION

After the abolition of slavery in Brazil, there was a demand for labor, particularly on coffee plantations. At the same time, Japan was facing issues with overpopulation and the government encouraged emigration to ease this pressure.

The first Japanese immigrants arrived in Brazil in 1908 as contract laborers who worked under harsh conditions, with another large wave arriving after World War II. Japanese immigrants went on to significantly enhance Brazil's agricultural development, introducing crops such as tea, strawberries, pumpkins, melons and persimmons, as well as advanced agricultural knowledge that played a crucial role in the development of rice and soybean cultivation.

Descendants of Japanese immigrants are called Nikkei and today Brazil is home to the largest Japanese community outside Japan. One of the biggest cultural hubs is the neighborhood of Liberdade, in São Paulo, which hosts the *Festa do Imigrante Japonês* (Japanese Immigrant Festival) annually.

Japanese cuisine has made a significant impact on Brazilian food culture. This can be seen most evidently in Kilo restaurants (traditional Brazilian buffet restaurants), which often have large and elaborate sushi displays, but also in the Japanese-Brazilian fusion restaurants in major cities like São Paulo, Paraná, Manaus and Rio de Janeiro.

Meat

Spatchcock chicken with dendê & coconut peppercorn sauce

This is hands down one of my favorite recipes in the book and it couldn't be simpler. It's inspired by the roast chicken curry in *MEZCLA* and also by my love of peppercorn sauce. My very untraditional version of the classic sauce has the added fruity, peppery notes of urucum (see page 23), creaminess from coconut milk and dendê and intensity from mustard, ginger and tomato. You'll want to drink the sauce straight from the tray, I promise.

Rather than describing how to spatchcock (or using pictures of a spreadeagled raw chicken), I suggest you look on YouTube or in my Instagram highlights for a tutorial, because it's much easier to learn by watching it being done. Alternatively, ask your butcher to do it for you and watch closely so you can do it yourself next time.

Serves 4 — GF
Prep time: 5–10 minutes
Cook time: 40 minutes
Marinade time: 1–3 hours or overnight
Rest time: 15 minutes

1 whole chicken (3 lb 12 oz/1.7 kg), spatchcocked
2 tsp rice vinegar
1 lime, halved
⅓ oz (10 g) freshly picked cilantro leaves
½ a yellow onion, peeled and thinly sliced

Marinade

¼ cup (60 g) yogurt
2 tsp medium curry powder
½ tsp ground urucum (aka annatto/achiote, see page 23 for alternatives)
¼ tsp sweet paprika (not smoked!)
1½ tsp fine sea salt
100 twists of freshly cracked pepper (½ tsp)

Curry sauce

1 × 14 oz (400 g) can of full-fat coconut milk
3 whole red bird's-eye chiles
⅓ cup (80 g) water
2 tbsp red palm oil (see page 20 for alternatives)
2 tbsp tomato paste
2 tbsp whole peppercorns (black or mixed)
1 tbsp English mustard
1 tbsp maple syrup
1 tbsp ginger–garlic mix (page 26)
100 twists of freshly cracked pepper (½ tsp)
1 tsp fine sea salt
¾ tsp ground urucum (aka annatto/achiote, see page 23)

Mix all the marinade ingredients together in a large bowl. Add the spatchcocked chicken, mix to coat thoroughly and leave to marinate for 1–3 hours at room temperature (or overnight, refrigerated, in which case bring to room temperature 2 hours before cooking).

Preheat the oven to 475°F (240°C).

Put all the curry sauce ingredients into an 11 × 14 in (27 × 37 cm) high-sided roasting pan and whisk everything together.

Place the chicken in the roasting pan skin side up, on top of the sauce. Spread the legs out so the skin browns evenly. Place on the rack in the lower third of the oven—you don't want it too near the top, as the fat will spit a bit.

Roast for 40 minutes, without opening the oven or basting, until the chicken is crispy and the sauce has thickened a bit.

Remove from the oven and let the chicken rest for 15 minutes before carving.

Stir the rice vinegar into the sauce. If the sauce sets a little, gently warm the pan on the stovetop, adding a splash of water to loosen if necessary.

Serve with the fresh lime, cilantro and onion.

Duck rice

This is inspired by *arroz de pato com tucupi*—duck rice in *tucupi*—a dish typical of the Amazonas and Pará states of Brazil. It's very similar to *pato no tucupi* (page 200), except that the duck is shredded into rice and it's less saucy. For the lack of *tucupi*, I've once again used my base of yellow tomatoes, garlic and ginger.

This recipe involves a few processes but it's well worth the effort. There are also lots of ways you can get ahead. The below can all be done up to 2 days before and kept refrigerated.

1. Cook the rice.
2. Roast and shred the duck.
3. Make the stock.
4. Make the tomato-ginger-garlic mixture.

To crisp up the duck skin before serving, bake in a preheated oven at 400°F (200°C) for about 5 minutes.

Serves 4
Prep time: 15 minutes
Soak time: 2 hours
Cook time: 2 hours 25 minutes

1 cup (250 g) short-grain brown rice
4 duck legs
fine sea salt
4¼ cups (1 kg) water
2–3 ripe golden/yellow tomatoes (1 lb 5 oz/600 g)
4 garlic cloves, peeled
⅓ oz (10 g) fresh ginger, peeled
1 bunch scallions, separated into white ends and green ends
3½ oz (100 g) watercress
⅓ oz (10 g) cilantro, thinly sliced
1½ tsp yellow chile mash (page 31)
1 lemon, halved
sea salt flakes
plenty of freshly cracked pepper

Spice rub

2 tsp fine sea salt
2 tsp ground coffee
1 tsp ground urucum (aka annatto/achiote, see page 23 for alternatives)
1 tsp Urfa pepper flakes
½ tsp ground cinnamon
½ tsp sweet paprika

Soak the rice in plenty of cold water for at least 2 hours or overnight.

Mix all the spice rub ingredients together in a large bowl. Use a sharp, pointed knife to poke holes all over the duck legs, then add them to the spice rub and mix to coat the legs thoroughly.

Place the legs skin side up in a baking dish that's just big enough to fit them in a single layer. You want them to be snug, but not on top of each other.

For the jus, mix together the guava juice, tamari and vinegar and pour it around the legs (try to avoid pouring it onto the skin).

Place the dish in a cold oven, then turn the oven on to 325°F (160°C) and roast for 2 hours, or until the meat is very soft and the skin is crispy.

Once the rice has soaked for at least 2 hours, drain and put it into a medium pot with 2 cups (500 g) of room-temperature water and ½ teaspoon of fine sea salt. Place on low heat, cover with a lid and cook for 35 minutes undisturbed. Remove from the heat and leave to rest for 10 minutes with the lid on, then remove the lid, mix and leave uncovered.

After 2 hours' roasting, remove the duck from the oven. Remove the skin and place it on a flat baking sheet, crispy side up. Pour the fat and jus from the baking dish into a sauté pan and set it aside.

Pull the meat off the bones onto a chopping board and roughly shred into large chunks.

To make the stock, place the bones in a pot and cover with 2 cups (500 g) water. Bring to a gentle simmer over medium heat.

recipe continues overleaf →

Duck jus

¾ cup (180 g) guava juice (see page 21)
1½ tbsp (25 g) tamari or soy sauce
2 tsp rice vinegar

Turn up the oven to 400°F (200°C).

Put the tomatoes, garlic, ginger and the white ends of the scallions into a food processor and pulse until very finely chopped. Transfer the mixture to the sauté pan containing the duck fat and jus. Place on medium–high heat and stir frequently for 10 minutes, or until the tomato mixture is golden brown. Add the shredded duck and cooked rice and stir-fry for 5 minutes, then add 1¼ cups (300 g) of the duck stock and cook for another 5 minutes, or until the broth has reduced and the rice is sticky and a little crispy in parts. Turn off the heat.

Place the pan of duck skin in the oven for 5 minutes, or until crisp.

Thinly slice the green ends of the scallions and add to the sauté pan along with the watercress, cilantro, yellow chile mash, the juice of a lemon and 1 teaspoon of sea salt flakes. Stir together.

Finish with a drizzle of oil, plenty of pepper and the crispy duck skin, broken into pieces.

Picadinho & sweet potato bake

Picadinho de carne moida is a simple spiced ground beef stew dish which I often turn to when I need a quick dinner. This simple version utilises a flavor-packed paste in the base, so there's no chopping involved.

Topped with grated sweet potato, which cooks into a layer that's soft beneath and crispy on top, this is a deliciously simple and crowd-pleasing meal in one.

Serves 6 — GF
Prep time: 10 minutes
Cook time: 1 hour

1 lb 3 oz (1 kg) ground beef
2 red romano peppers, deseeded and finely chopped
2 lb (900 g) sweet potatoes, peeled and roughly grated
3 tbsp olive oil
½ tsp fine sea salt
1 oz (30 g) Parmesan, finely grated
scant ½ cup (100 g) yogurt, to serve
1 lime, halved, to serve

Umami paste

2 yellow onions, peeled and roughly chopped (8 oz/240 g)
8 garlic cloves (1 oz/25 g), peeled
4 mild red chiles, deseeded and roughly chopped
⅔ cup (160 g) tomato paste
generous ½ cup (120 g) olive oil
1½ oz (40 g) dried mixed/wild mushrooms
1 tbsp rice vinegar
1 tbsp Worcestershire sauce
2½ tsp fine sea salt
2 tsp ground cumin
1 tsp curry powder
½ tsp ground cinnamon
¼ tsp ground allspice
a good grating of nutmeg
about 100 twists of freshly cracked pepper (½ tsp)

Preheat the oven to 475°F (240°C).

Put all the umami paste ingredients into a food processor and blend until smooth, scraping down the sides as needed.

Put the paste into a 12 in (30 cm) Dutch oven or ovenproof pot, for which you have a lid (or a similar-sized baking pan), along with the ground beef and chopped peppers. Mix very well, then bake for 20 minutes until browned and bubbling.

Break up the beef, mix again and return to the oven for 10 minutes.

In a large bowl, mix the grated sweet potato with 2 tablespoons of olive oil and ½ teaspoon of fine sea salt, then spread out over the beef. Cover with a lid (or foil) and bake for 20 minutes.

Remove from the oven and turn the broiler to the highest setting.

Drizzle the surface evenly with the remaining tablespoon of olive oil, then scatter over the Parmesan.

Place under the broiler for 10 minutes, or until crisp and browned—use a blowtorch if your broiler isn't particularly powerful.

Drizzle with oil and serve with the yogurt and fresh lime.

Chicken livers with urucum, paprika & coffee butter

Brazil has a nose-to-tail cooking culture and when it comes to chicken, you'll find feet in stocks and stews, hearts threaded onto skewers in *churrascarias* and pan-fried and stuffed into sandwiches in *botecos*. My favorite chicken offal is liver and here I've paired it with an urucum (see page 23) and coffee butter, maple and citrus juice. I like to spoon the livers and sauce onto grilled bread and top with fresh herbs, onions and chile vinegar.

Another option for this recipe is to turn it into pâté—just blend the whole thing once you've completed step 5 and serve with the same condiments.

Churrascaria—A grill restaurant serving a variety of meats on skewers. Boteco—A casual local bar that serves drinks, snacks and comfort food.

Serves 4 as an appetizer	GF
Prep time: 5 minutes	
Cook time: 5 minutes	
Marinade time: 30 minutes–1 hour	

10½ oz (300 g) chicken livers, at room temperature
1 lemon, halved
1 lime, halved
1 tbsp maple syrup
sea salt flakes
a good pinch of Urfa pepper flakes

Marinade

3 whole red bird's-eye chiles
2 tsp olive oil
¾ tsp fine sea salt
½ tsp ground urucum (aka annatto/achiote, see page 23 for alternatives)
½ tsp ground coffee
¼ tsp garlic powder
50 twists of freshly cracked pepper (¼ tsp)

Butter

2 tbsp salted butter
2 tbsp olive oil
2 tsp tomato paste
1 garlic clove, peeled and very finely chopped
½ tsp sweet paprika (not smoked)

To serve

⅛ oz (5 g) fresh parsley, picked but with some stalks left on
⅛ oz (5 g) cilantro, picked but with some stalks left on
½ a small yellow onion, peeled and thinly sliced
chile vinegar or hot sauce

Rinse and drain the livers to remove any blood, then *thoroughly* pat them dry with paper towels. Remove any connective tissues. Put the livers into a bowl with all the marinade ingredients and mix well. Leave to marinate for 30 minutes to 1 hour at room temperature.

Put all the butter ingredients into a small bowl and set aside.

Place a nonstick frying pan on high heat. Once the pan is very hot, add the livers and the chiles, spaced apart as much as possible. Fry until nicely charred on the bottom, about 2½ minutes. Turn the livers over and fry for another 1 minute on the other side.

Turn the heat down to low, then add the butter ingredients and gently fry, swirling the pan until the ingredients meld together, about 1½ minutes. Squeeze over the juice of 1 lemon and ½ a lime and swirl to incorporate it into the sauce.

Remove from the heat, add the maple syrup and swirl the pan again. Season with sea salt flakes, plenty of pepper and a sprinkle of Urfa pepper flakes.

Transfer to a platter and top with the herbs, onion slices and a good squeeze of lime. I like to drizzle the livers with chile vinegar or hot sauce. You can also chop up the chiles in the sauce for extra heat, if you like.

ITALIAN IMMIGRATION

The unification of Italy in the 1860s led to socio-economic changes that created challenges for many rural Italians, especially Calabrians and Sicilians. During this time, Brazil was experiencing a labor shortage in the agricultural sector and actively encouraged immigration, offering opportunities in coffee plantations, industry and urban centers.

Today, Brazil has the largest diaspora of Italians outside Brazil, with an estimated 30 million people of Italian descent who have contributed significantly to the cultural landscape.

Italian food, especially pasta, pizza and polenta, has become a staple in Brazilian cuisine, but a hybrid of Italian and Brazilian cooking has also emerged. For example, a popular topping/filling for both pizza and *lasanha* is "*frango com catupiry*," a combination of shredded chicken, *catupiry* (a Brazilian cheese spread) and corn that Italian purists would probably find quite alarming. In Brazil, *lasanha* is also often topped with *batata palha* (fried potato sticks).

Italy's best contribution to Brazilian cuisine, in my opinion, is sausages. The Brazilian "*Calabresa*" sausage is modeled after the chunky, flavorful, spiced sausages of Calabria. You can find a recipe inspired by *Calabresa* sausages, with a few Ixta twists, on page 226.

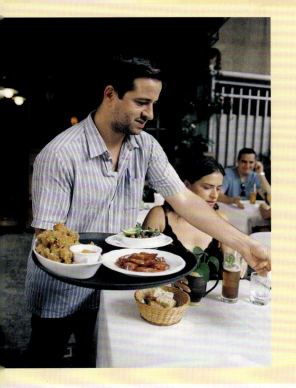

Guava, curry & chile meatballs

If you've ever tried *Calabresa* sausages in Brazil—which are modeled on Calabrian sausages—you'll know that they are superior to just about any other sausage out there (don't get me started on my contempt for English sausages, which lack flavor and texture and are always filled to the brim with rusk and fillers). Fresh *Calabresa* sausages are hard to come by (unless you can get to a Brazilian butcher), which is why I've come up with these meatballs. Just like Italian and Brazilian sausages, they are packed full of flavor and have a chunky texture.

I've added a few of my favorite untraditional flavors here—guava jam, curry powder, Scotch bonnet and mustard—and the result is sweet, sticky and completely addictive.

These meatballs go incredibly well with the *feijão* (page 88) and the Blood oranges with chile ginger–garlic oil (page 80). You could also shape them into patties and serve them in buns with a zingy herb and onion salad, or with fried eggs.

Serves 4 — GF
Prep time: 5 minutes
Cook time: 9 minutes

- 14 oz (400 g) ground pork (not lean!)
- 5 oz (140 g) pancetta or lardons (chopped into roughly ¼ in/½ cm cubes)
- 3 tbsp guava jam (or another tropical jam like mango or pineapple)
- 1½ tbsp chopped red chile condiment (page 29, or use a store-bought chopped chile condiment)
- 2 tsp tomato paste
- 2 tsp English mustard
- 1 garlic clove, crushed
- ½ tbsp olive oil, plus extra for shaping and frying
- 1 tsp rice vinegar
- 1½ tsp medium curry powder
- ¾ tsp fine sea salt
- ¼ tsp ground allspice
- about 30 twists of of freshly cracked pepper (⅛ tsp)

Preheat the oven to 410°F (210°C).

Put all the ingredients into a large bowl and mix until thoroughly combined—make sure you incorporate the guava jam, tomato paste and mustard thoroughly.

With lightly oiled hands, form into 8 meatballs, squeezing as you go so that they are compact.

Heat a large frying pan on high heat. Once hot, fry, turning, until crisp and well browned all over—about 4 minutes. Transfer to a baking pan and finish cooking in the oven for 5 minutes.

Serve the meatballs with the feijão (page 88), with salad or in a sandwich.

Picanha with charred chile, garlic & lime butter

Picanha is the cut of beef that Brazil is best known for—it's the sirloin cap, with the fat cap left on. It may look like a dauntingly large piece of meat to get right, but follow these steps closely and you'll get great results.

The combination of coffee, chile and urucum (see page 230) in the marinade creates a great crust on the meat as well as a deliciously smoky flavor. The marinade does tend to burn a bit (this creates flavor!) so make sure you open the windows and turn on your extraction fan when searing the steak.

The cooking time I've included is for medium–rare (leaning towards rare) steak. Cook for 5–10 minutes longer per side for medium. Picanha can be difficult to find, so, on the opposite page, I've provided instructions for cooking a 1 lb 3 oz (1 kg) sirloin steak (a large, sharing-sized cut). Overleaf, you'll find a recipe for individual sirloin steaks.

Serves 4 — GF
Prep time: 5 minutes
Cook time: 40–42 minutes
Marinade time: 2 hours
Rest time: 20 minutes

1 lb 3 oz (1 kg) picanha (sirloin cap with the fat cap left on)
fine sea salt
1 lime, to serve

Marinade

1 tbsp olive oil
½ tbsp maple syrup
¾ tsp ground coffee
¾ tsp Urfa pepper flakes
¾ tsp ground urucum (aka annatto/achiote, see page 23 for alternatives)
50 twists of freshly cracked pepper (¼ tsp)

Butter

1 red chile
1 Scotch bonnet (optional, add less or use a milder chile if you prefer)
3 garlic cloves
10½ tbsp (150 g) salted butter, softened
1 tsp lime zest
½ tsp Urfa pepper flakes
½ tsp red pepper paste (or tomato paste)
½ tsp sea salt flakes

Pat the steak dry with paper towels, then generously salt on all sides, including the fat. Mix together the ingredients for the marinade, then rub the marinade all over the flesh sides (not on the fat side). Leave to marinate for 2 hours at room temperature.

Open the windows and turn on your extraction fan.

Preheat the oven to 350°F (180°C).

Place the picanha fat side down in a large, cool cast-iron pan and turn the heat to medium–low.

Place a heavy pan on top of the steak to weigh it down. Gently fry for 10–12 minutes, to render the fat and get a dark crust on the fat side. Carefully spoon away the fat as it renders.

Set a rack over a roasting pan. Place the steak on the rack, fat side up. Transfer to the oven for 30 minutes, or until a meat thermometer pierced into the thickest part of the meat reads 130°F (55°C). Remove from the oven and rest for 20 minutes.

While the picanha is cooking, make the butter. Place a small frying pan on high heat. Add the chile, Scotch bonnet (if using) and garlic cloves and cook until nicely charred all over, 2–3 minutes on each side. Transfer to a bowl and cover with a plate to soften.

Deseed and destalk the chiles, then put the chiles and garlic into the small bowl of a food processor along with all the remaining butter ingredients (add the chile in stages if you like, to get the desired heat level). Blend until smooth and combined, scraping down the sides as needed.

Slice the steak against the grain (see intro overleaf) and season with sea salt flakes. Serve with the chile butter, fresh lime juice and salad.

See page 231 for a recipe photo. →

Cooking instructions for a large, 1 lb 3 oz (1 kg) sirloin steak (serves 4)

Preheat the oven to 350°F (180°C).

Marinate the steak as per the recipe on the opposite page.

Heat a large pan on high heat. Once very hot, place the steak in the pan fat strip down, holding it up with tongs. Render the fat until well browned, 2½–3 minutes.

Pour away the fat, then sear the steak for about 1 minute per side, to get a nice browned crust.

Place on a baking sheet and transfer to the oven for 6 minutes, then flip over and cook for another 6 minutes (for medium–rare, cook a little longer, if you prefer).

Transfer to a board and rest for 15–20 minutes. Slice against the grain, sprinkle with sea salt flakes and serve with the chile butter and fresh lime.

Quick steaks with coffee & chile butter

After I developed the recipe for the picanha on page 228, it occurred to me that people hardly ever cook such a large/expensive cut of meat, so I thought it would be useful to provide a quick version of that recipe using smaller steaks and a quicker butter that doesn't involve a food processor.

To "slice against the grain," look at the meat and observe the lines or strands running through it—these are the muscle fibers, or the "grain." Position your knife (make sure it's nice and sharp) so that you cut across these lines, rather than along them. By cutting against the grain, you shorten the muscle fibers, which makes the meat feel softer and easier to chew.

Serves 2 — GF
Prep time: 5 minutes
Cook time: 4½ minutes
Rest time: 8 minutes

2 × 8 oz (220 g) sirloin steaks
fine sea salt
2 tbsp salted butter
⅛ oz (5 g) scallion green ends, very finely chopped (use the whites in another recipe)
⅛ oz (5 g) cilantro, very finely chopped
2 limes, halved
sea salt flakes

Marinade

1 tbsp mild olive oil
½ tbsp maple syrup
¾ tsp ground coffee
¾ tsp Urfa pepper flakes
¾ tsp ground urucum (aka annatto/achiote, see page 23)
50 twists of freshly cracked pepper (¼ tsp)

Bring the steak to room temperature 1 hour before cooking. Pat dry with paper towels, then generously season both sides with fine sea salt.

Mix all the marinade ingredients together, then use enough of the marinade to coat both sides of the steak (you won't need it all—keep the rest for the sauce).

Open the windows and turn on your extraction fan.

Heat a large frying pan on high heat. Once the pan is very hot, place the steaks in the pan, spaced apart, and cook for 2½ minutes. Flip the steaks over and cook for another 2 minutes.

Transfer to a board to rest for 8 minutes while you prep the butter.

Remove the pan from the heat and leave to cool for a few minutes. Add the butter, scallion greens, cilantro, the juice of 1 lime and the remaining marinade to the pan and swirl, letting the butter melt in the residual heat.

Slice the steak against the grain (see intro) and plate. Sprinkle with sea salt flakes, then spoon over the butter.

Serve with the remaining lime.

Left Quick steaks with coffee & chile butter
Right Picanha with charred chile, garlic & lime butter

Mango, ginger & lemon sorbet

Both of these sorbets are made with frozen fresh fruit—no ice-cream churner required—which is my preferred method of making sorbets, as it really showcases the flavor of the fruit and requires minimal added sugar.

I encourage you to use this sorbet-making method with other fruit, just make sure they're nice and ripe. Papaya, plums, berries, peaches, apricots, melons and pineapples all work well, but the possibilities are truly endless. You can also experiment with your flavorings: add fresh or dried chile, herbs like basil, cilantro or mint, spices like cinnamon, nutmeg or black pepper. You could also infuse tea (I love rooibos tea) into the ginger syrup/honey or alcohol before adding.

Serves 6   GF, V, VG
Prep time: 5–10 minutes
Freezing time: overnight plus 3–4 hours

- 4 extra ripe Alphonso mangoes
- 3½ tbsp lemon juice, plus extra to serve
- 1½ oz (40 g) stem ginger (or peeled fresh ginger)
- 2 tbsp stem ginger syrup (or honey, maple syrup or agave syrup)
- 2 tbsp cachaça or mezcal, plus extra to serve (optional)

Peel the mangoes and remove the pits. Cut into random pieces (you should have about 1 lb 8 oz/680 g) and transfer to a wide container, along with all the pulp and juice on your chopping board. Freeze overnight (or until frozen solid).

Once frozen solid, break up the mango into roughly 1½ in (4 cm) chunks. Put into a food processor with all of the remaining ingredients and blend until completely smooth, scraping down the sides as needed. Taste—you may want to add more sweetness and/or acidity depending on the ripeness of your mangoes.

Return to the container and freeze until set but scoopable, 3–4 hours.

Serve with a squeeze of lemon and a splash of cachaça or mezcal.

Guava, cinnamon, strawberry & lime sorbet

Serves 6   GF, V, VGO
Prep time: 5 minutes
Freezing time: overnight plus 3–4 hours

- 2½ cups (600 g) guava juice or purée
- 7 oz (200 g) ripe strawberries
- 2½ tbsp honey (or maple/agave syrup)
- 3½ tbsp lime juice, plus extra to serve
- 2 tbsp cachaça or mezcal, plus extra to serve
- 2 tsp vanilla bean paste
- ½ tsp ground cinnamon
- 50 twists of freshly cracked pepper (¼ tsp)

Pour the guava juice into ice trays and freeze overnight (or until frozen solid).

Remove the stalks from the strawberries, then roughly chop. Place in a wide container and freeze overnight (or until frozen solid).

Put the frozen guava juice cubes and strawberries into a food processor along with all of the remaining ingredients. Process until completely smooth, scraping down the sides as needed, then transfer to a container and freeze until set but scoopable, 3–4 hours.

Serve with a squeeze of lime and a splash of cachaça or mezcal.

See page 236 and 237 for a recipe photo. →

Note
Once frozen solid, transfer to the fridge for 30 minutes before scooping.

Top Left Papaya, lime & chile granita
Bottom Left Guava, cinnamon, strawberry & lime sorbet
Top Right Mango, ginger & lemon sorbet
Bottom Right Roasted banana ice cream with chocolate fudge sauce

Papaya, lime & chile granita

This granita is the ultimate zingy refresher—thank you to my dearest Flik Davis for creating this deliciously easy recipe to cool us down on a very hot book shoot day.

Serves 6 — GF, V, VG
Prep time: 5 minutes
Freezing time: overnight

- 1 large extra ripe papaya (3 lb/1.4 kg)
- ⅔ cup (150 g) mezcal or cachaça
- scant ½ cup (100 g) lime juice (5–6 small limes)
- ¼ cup (70 g) maple syrup, plus extra to serve
- 1 tsp Aleppo pepper flakes (or ¼ tsp regular chile flakes)
- ½ tsp sea salt flakes

To serve
- fresh lime
- sea salt flakes
- Aleppo pepper flakes

Halve the papaya and remove the seeds with a spoon. Scoop the ripe flesh out into a blender (you should have about 1 lb 13 oz/840 g) and add the mezcal, lime juice, maple syrup, Aleppo pepper flakes and sea salt flakes. Taste—you may want to add more sweetness and/or acidity depending on the sweetness and flavor of your papaya.

Pour into a wide container and freeze overnight until set.

Scrape the surface with a spoon or fork to create the granita and transform the icy layers into fluffy crystals.

Serve in bowls, topped with a squeeze of fresh lime, a sprinkle of sea salt flakes and Aleppo pepper flakes, and a drizzle of maple syrup if needed. You can also add a splash more booze if you like.

See page 237 for a recipe photo. →

Roasted banana ice cream with chocolate fudge sauce

This ice cream is vegan, dairy-free and gluten-free (as long as you use gluten-free miso), so it's great if you're catering for people with different dietary requirements. It's also very fun to put together—set out the ice cream, fudge sauce and chopped nuts and let everyone create their own sundae!

Another alternative for the fudge sauce is to turn it into truffles. If you continue to cook the sauce until it's as thick as butterscotch, then chill it until completely set, you can roll it in cocoa powder, shredded coconut or chocolate sprinkles and you'll have yourself a much less sweet version of *brigadeiros*, the classic Brazilian chocolate truffles made with condensed milk.

Serves 4   GF, V, VG

Prep time: 10 minutes
Cook time: 49–54 minutes
Freezing time: overnight plus 6 hours

Ice cream

5 extra ripe bananas, peeled and roughly chopped (1 lb 3 oz/540g)
½ cup (150 g) maple syrup
¾ cup (200 g) coconut cream (you'll need another ¾ cup/200 g for the sauce)
1½ tbsp white miso paste
1 tsp vanilla bean paste
½ tsp instant coffee powder
1¾ oz (50 g) dark chocolate, very finely chopped

Spiced caramelized nuts

scant 1 cup (100 g) pistachio kernels, shelled
¾ cup (100 g) whole hazelnuts
2 tbsp light brown sugar
1½ tbsp maple syrup
2 tsp mild olive oil
½ tsp ground coffee
¼ tsp fine sea salt
freshly cracked pepper

Chocolate fudge sauce

¾ cup (200 g) coconut cream
⅓ cup (100 g) maple syrup
2 tbsp cocoa powder (100% cocoa solids)
1 tsp vanilla bean paste
1½ tsp white miso paste
½ tsp instant coffee powder (or coffee grounds)
¼ tsp ground cinnamon

See page 237 for a recipe photo. →

Preheat the oven to 410°F (210°C).

Line a baking dish with parchment paper, then place the bananas and maple syrup in the dish. Mix and bake for 25–30 minutes, gently stirring halfway, until the bananas are soft and browned and the syrup has reduced a little. Leave to cool, then lift the parchment paper, along with the bananas and syrup, into a container and freeze overnight.

Lower the heat to 350°F (180°C).

Chop the nuts roughly into halves (you want nice chunks, so don't chop them too much). Line a baking sheet with parchment paper. Put the nuts on the pan along with the sugar, maple syrup, oil, coffee, salt and pepper and mix well. Bake for about 17 minutes, stirring halfway, until well browned. Set aside to cool, break the clumps of nuts apart, then store in an airtight container.

The next day, break up the frozen banana and solidified maple syrup and put into a food processor or blender with the coconut cream, miso, vanilla and coffee. Blend until completely smooth, scraping down the sides as needed. Transfer to a container and freeze for 2 hours, or until set but still soft. At this point, fold in the chocolate, then return to the freezer until set but still scoopable—about another 4 hours.

Put all the fudge sauce ingredients into a medium pot and whisk until smooth. Place on medium heat and cook, stirring often, until thickened to a pourable fudge sauce consistency, about 7 minutes (it will thicken more as it cools).

Serve the ice cream with the warm fudge sauce and the spiced nut crumbs.

Notes
The roasted banana will need to freeze overnight, and then you'll need another 4 hours to freeze the ice cream once it's been blended, so make sure to factor that in.

Once the ice cream has frozen solid it will need about 40 minutes at room temperature to come back to scooping consistency before serving.

MEMORIES OF FAMILY AND FOOD

I often say my brain works in food. My memory is patchy, except when it comes to flavors: I'm not particularly observant, unless there's food involved. It's no surprise, then, that my favorite family stories revolve around food and I remember family members I've never met via the dishes they loved or foods they made.

In the introduction, I touched upon the kitchens of my great-grandmothers. Vovó Iracema loved to spoon freshly churned *nata* (cream) over her *feijão* (black beans), while Vovó Eugênia adored savory crêpes filled with spiced meat, topped with fresh tomato sauce and cilantro (see my version on page 209).

And then there are my mother's grandfathers. Vovô Vitorino had a special love for *abacatada*—a creamy avocado smoothie made with condensed milk— with which he ended every meal.

When my mother or her siblings were unwell, Vovô Sandoval would painstakingly scoop out the flesh of apples, creating a purée to comfort them with.

My mother's great-aunt, Tia Jacyra, was famous throughout Natal for her *doces de fruta*—delicious fruit sweets. My mother vividly remembers her kitchen overflowing with crates of vibrant, tropical fruits: *coco verde, mamão, jabuticaba, goiaba, carambola, maracujá, manga*. Huge pots simmered on the stove, filling the air with sweet, tropical aromas, while her marble counters were neatly lined with jars of irresistibly colorful, tempting sweets.

Tia Dedé, on the other hand, was famous for her *recheio de canudinho*—delicate pastry horns inspired by Sicilian cannoli, filled with both sweet and savory delights. My mother's favorite dessert was *cartola*, a north-eastern delicacy of fried bananas spiced with cinnamon and topped with freshly grilled cheese and Tia Dedé made the very best version of it.

Coconut rice pudding with guava-strawberry jam

In Brazil, *arroz doce* (literally "sweet rice," but it refers to rice pudding) is simply made with white rice, milk, sugar and sometimes a bit of cinnamon.

I'm using my favorite short-grain brown rice here instead; I love its texture and nutty flavor. I also use coconut milk instead of regular milk or cream to make things lighter and more aromatic.

The rice pudding itself isn't particularly sweet, but once you swirl in the jam and top with brown sugar, I think it's perfectly balanced. I like to serve it warm, with cold coconut yogurt.

I use the guava-strawberry jam a few times throughout the book—in the pastéis on page 250 and the corn cake on page 260. The jam keeps in the fridge for up to two weeks and one batch will be enough for two different recipes.

Serves 6	GF, V, VGO
Prep time: 10 minutes	
Cook time: 1 hour	
Soaking: overnight	

Rice pudding

1½ cups (300 g) short-grain brown rice, soaked overnight
2 × 14 oz (400 g) cans of full-fat coconut milk
2 cups (500 g) cold water
⅓ cup (100 g) honey (or maple/agave syrup)
1 cup (90 g) unsweetened shredded coconut
¾ oz (20 g) fresh ginger, roughly chopped
2 tsp vanilla bean paste
2 cinnamon sticks
⅛ tsp ground allspice or cloves
½ tsp fine sea salt

Guava strawberry jam

1 lb (500 g) ripe strawberries, stalks removed and roughly chopped
1⅔ cups (400 g) guava juice or purée (try to find one with as little sugar as possible)
2 tsp honey (or maple/agave syrup)
1 lime, halved

To serve

brown sugar
ground cinnamon
coconut or regular yogurt

Soak the rice overnight in plenty of water. Don't skip this step or the rice won't cook evenly.

Drain and rinse.

Put the drained rice into a 10 in (25 cm) pot, for which you have a lid, with all the remaining ingredients for the rice pudding. Mix well.

Place on the lowest heat, cover with a lid and cook for 1 hour, undisturbed. Don't be tempted to remove the lid to check the rice, or you'll release the steam and pressure in the pan. After 1 hour, remove the lid, remove the cinnamon sticks and ginger and stir well.

While the rice is cooking, make the jam. Add all the ingredients to a 10 in (25 cm) wide pot and place on high heat. Bring to a rolling simmer and cook, stirring often, until reduced to a loose jam consistency, 20–30 minutes. Set aside to cool a little.

Spoon the warm rice pudding into bowls and swirl in some jam. Top with a generous amount of brown sugar and a good sprinkle of ground cinnamon. Finish with a spoonful of cold coconut yogurt and serve.

Plantain fritters with warm chocolate fudge sauce

These fritters are very loosely inspired by *bolinho de chuva*—raindrop-shaped Brazilian doughnuts with cinnamon sugar.

This recipe might seem a little long but it's actually incredibly easy. You must use ripe plantains—they should be yellow, quite soft and with plenty of black marks (overripe bananas will work too).

My mom is a nutritionist with a pretty severe gluten intolerance and therefore we grew up in a predominantly gluten-free household. Because of this, my default is to make recipes gluten-free so my mom can eat them too (especially in this instance, as she is *obsessed* with plantain).

For this recipe I use chickpea flour, which has a pretty weird taste when it's raw but works incredibly well when fried. What's more, the chickpea flour makes the fritters even more yellow, which is aesthetically very pleasing, contrasted with the brown of the chocolate sauce.

Makes 15 GF, V, VG
Prep time: 5–10 minutes
Cook time: 33–43 minutes

4¼ cups (1 liter) light olive oil, for frying

Fritters

2–4 small, ripe plantains (1 lb 11 oz/760 g—they should be soft and covered in black spots)
1⅔ cups (140 g) chickpea flour
⅓ cup (60 g) sugar (preferably organic)
¼ cup (30 g) cornstarch
5 tsp baking powder
zest of 2 tangerines
1 tsp vanilla bean paste
½ tsp ground cinnamon
½ tsp ground ginger
½ tsp fine sea salt

Cinnamon sugar

generous ⅓ cup (75 g) sugar (preferably organic)
½ tsp ground cinnamon
plenty of freshly cracked pepper

Chocolate fudge sauce

1 × 14 oz (400 g) can of full-fat coconut milk
¾ cup (250 g) maple syrup
¼ cup (30 g) cocoa powder (100% cocoa solids)
heaped 1 tbsp white miso paste
2 tsp vanilla bean paste
2 tsp instant coffee powder
¼ tsp ground cinnamon

See page 248 for a recipe photo. →

Peel the plantains and put them into a large bowl. Mash them thoroughly until smooth (you should have about 15½ oz/440 g). Add the rest of the fritter ingredients and stir to combine, ensuring there are no clumps of flour or plantain. Set aside.

Put all the cinnamon sugar ingredients into a medium bowl and mix together.

Put all the fudge sauce ingredients into a medium saucepan and whisk until smooth. Place on medium heat and cook, whisking often, until the mixture bubbles away, reduces and thickens to a dipping fudge sauce consistency (this can take anywhere between 15 and 25 minutes). Remove from the heat.

Fill a medium pot with oil so it's three-quarters full. Place on medium–low heat until the oil reaches 325°F (170°C).

Place a rack on a baking sheet. Preheat the oven to 375°F (190°C).

Once the oil is at temperature, use a regular cutlery spoon to carefully drop in spoonfuls of batter—you should be able to fry 4 or 5 at a time. Cook for 3½ minutes, turning the fritters every now and then, until crisp and golden brown all over. If they are coloring straight away or getting very dark, turn the heat all the way down or remove the pan from the heat for a few minutes.

Once ready, use a slotted spoon to transfer the fritters to the rack. Once all the fritters are cooked, transfer the baking sheet to the oven for 3 minutes. Break one fritter open to make sure it's cooked all the way through—if not, return them to the oven for a few minutes.

Add the fritters to the cinnamon sugar bowl and toss to coat.

Gently warm the sauce and serve alongside the fritters.

Note
You can use regular all-purpose flour if you don't need these to be GF.

Guava & cheese pastéis

In Brazil, *Romeu e Julieta* refers not only to Shakespeare's young lovers but also to the combination of cheese with *goiabada* (guava paste).

In its simplest form, *queijo Minas*, an unpasteurised cow's cheese from Minas Gerais, is simply served alongside guava paste, but you can make anything from cakes, pastries, cheesecakes and pancakes to ice creams based on this combination.

These *pastéis* are somewhere in between sweet and salty, not a dessert as such but a great afternoon treat with some black coffee. You can use the pastry to make larger galettes; try a version using the cheese mixture on the bottom and cover with a layer of sliced bananas. Top with maple syrup, coarse brown sugar and cinnamon before baking.

Makes 16   V
Prep time: 15 minutes
Cook time: 40–45 minutes
Chill time: 2 hours
Cool time: 10 minutes

Crunchy spelt pastry

all-purpose flour, for dusting

6 tbsp (90 g) unsalted butter, cut into 1 in (3 cm) cubes and frozen

1¼ cups (120 g) spelt flour (or all-purpose flour)

¼ cup (40 g) quick-cook polenta

¼ cup (50 g) light brown sugar

¼ tsp fine sea salt

about 20 twists of freshly cracked pepper (⅛ tsp)

½ tsp smoked red pepper flakes (such as Urfa or chipotle)

1½ tbsp olive oil

3 tbsp ice-cold water

Cheese mix

scant ½ cup (100 g) yogurt

3½ oz (100 g) feta

½ cup (100 g) ricotta

Guava-strawberry jam

1 lb (500 g) ripe strawberries, stalks removed and roughly chopped

1⅔ cups (400 g) guava juice or purée (try to find one with as little sugar as possible)

2 tsp honey (or maple/agave syrup)

1 lime, halved

Plus

1 egg, beaten

demerara or coarse brown sugar

Put all the pastry ingredients into a food processor and pulse a few times until the butter is in small pieces. Tip onto a clean surface and form into a flat 4 in (10 cm) square. Wrap in plastic wrap and freeze.

For the jam, add all the ingredients to a 10 in (25 cm) wide pot and place on high heat. Bring to a rolling simmer and cook, stirring often, until reduced to a loose jam consistency, 20–30 minutes. Set aside to cool a little.

Dust your work surface with plenty of all-purpose flour, then unwrap the pastry onto it. Roll the pastry out into a 12 in (30 cm) square, flouring the rolling pin, pastry and surface as needed so the pastry doesn't stick.

Fold into thirds, then fold into thirds again. Roll out the pastry, flouring the rolling pin and your surface as you go. Repeat these steps three more times—so your pastry ends up with lots of layers—ending up with a 4 in (10 cm) square. Wrap in plastic wrap and chill for 2 hours.

In a medium bowl, mix the yogurt, feta and ricotta together and set aside.

Preheat the oven to 425°F (220°C). Line a baking sheet with parchment paper.

Remove the pastry from the fridge and roll out into a thin rectangle, about 2 mm thick. Use an 4 in (11 cm) round pastry cutter to cut out as many circles as possible, placing them on the lined baking sheet. Gather the remaining pastry together, re-roll and cut into more circles. You should end up with 16.

Spread 1 tablespoon of the cheese mixture in the center of each pastry circle, leaving ¾ in (2 cm) free around the edge.

Spoon a few teaspoons of jam on top of the cheese mixture, then fold over and crimp the edges as in the photo opposite. Brush the edges of the pastry with beaten egg, then sprinkle with demerara or coarse brown sugar.

Bake for 10 minutes, then rotate the pan and bake for another 10 minutes, until the pastry is crisp and golden. Cool for 10 minutes before serving.

Top Left Spiced chocolate torte
Bottom Left Bolo de macaxeira, coco e maracuja
Top Right Papaya & chocolate cake with citrus honey glaze
Bottom Right Pineapple torte

Pineapple torte

This is inspired by my banana and sesame cake in *MEZCLA*, in that it's made with mostly fruit and hardly any flour, sugar and butter. I've called it a torte rather than a cake, as it's soft and pudding-y on the inside from all the fruit, rather than spongy, and crispy and sticky around the edges.

You *must* use a ripe pineapple for this—it should be a little soft and you should be able to smell a strong pineapple fragrance through the skin. This might mean that you have to let it ripen for a few days after you've bought it, but trust me, it will be worth the wait. If it's not ripe, the fruit won't soften enough during baking.

I've used whole-grain spelt flour, but you could use all-purpose flour if you prefer.

You'll only use half a pineapple in this recipe—any more would make the batter too wet—but you can use the other half to make pineapple pimenta (page 30).

Serves 6   V
Prep time: 5–10 minutes
Cook time: 50 minutes
Cool time: 2 hours

1 whole, very ripe pineapple (see intro)
2 tbsp demerara or coarse brown sugar

Batter

3 tbsp honey (or maple/agave syrup)
3½ tbsp ghee (from a jar, not a can), softened or melted and cooled (or cooled melted butter)
⅔ cup (60 g) ground almonds
scant ½ cup (40 g) whole-grain spelt flour (or all-purpose flour)
1 large egg
zest of 1 lime
1 tsp vanilla bean paste
¼ tsp ground ginger
¼ tsp ground cinnamon
⅛ tsp fine sea salt

Preheat the oven to 400°F (200°C). Line and lightly grease an 8 in (20 cm) cake pan.

Peel the pineapple, then halve lengthways (you'll only need half a pineapple, see intro). Place the pineapple half on a board, cut side down. Halve again lengthways (see the photo overleaf), then cut diagonally to remove the core. Cut into ⅛ in (4 mm) slices. Place the slices in a sieve to drain off excess juice (otherwise the batter will be too wet).

Put all the batter ingredients into a large bowl and whisk until smooth and combined.

Once the pineapple has drained, add the pineapple slices (you should have about 12½ oz/360 g) to the batter and fold everything together so the slices are coated in batter. Be very gentle and try not to break up the pineapple pieces.

Spoon into the prepared pan and push down to create a level surface. Sprinkle the sugar evenly over. Bake for 25 minutes, then rotate the pan and bake for another 25 minutes, or until crisp and golden brown on top.

Leave to cool for at least 2 hours in the pan before serving. This is *very* important, as the torte needs to set completely before slicing. Store at room temperature in an airtight container for up to 2 days.

Papaya & chocolate cake with citrus honey glaze

This cake is inspired by the classic *bolo de cenoura com chocolate*—carrot cake with a chocolate glaze—a very popular dessert in Brazil in which all the ingredients are blended in a blender, carrots and all.

This version uses ripe papaya instead of carrot and with the aim of creating a healthy-ish cake, I use ghee instead of the traditional vegetable oil, brown sugar instead of white sugar and ground almonds instead of flour. I've also added citrus zest and spices to give it a little complexity, as well as a citrus honey glaze. It's incredibly simple to make, gluten-free and the result is deliciously moist and fruity.

Serves 6 — GF, V
Prep time: 10 minutes
Cook time: 48 minutes

Batter

½ cup (100 g) ghee (from a jar, not a can) or butter
1 very-ripe papaya (1 lb/450 g)
3 large eggs
2⅔ cups (220 g) ground almonds
scant ½ cup (80 g) light brown sugar
zest of 2 tangerines (save the juice for the glaze)
zest of 1 lemon (save the juice for the glaze)
1 tsp baking powder
1 tsp vanilla bean paste
½ tsp ground ginger
¼ tsp ground cinnamon
¼ tsp fine sea salt

Glaze

juice of 2 tangerines
juice of 1 lemon
2½ tbsp honey (or maple/agave syrup)

Choc topping

5 tbsp (70 g) full-fat coconut milk (from a carton, not a can)
¼ cup (70 g) maple syrup
½ cup (50 g) cocoa powder (100% cocoa solids)
⅛ tsp fine sea salt

Preheat the oven to 350°F (180°C). Line and grease an 8 in (20 cm) cake pan.

Melt the ghee or butter in a small saucepan, then leave to cool for a few minutes.

Remove the skin and seeds from the papaya and roughly chop—you want 9 oz (250 g) of peeled flesh (don't use any more or the batter will be too wet).

Add the cooled, melted ghee to a blender or food processor along with the chopped papaya and all the remaining batter ingredients.

Blend until smooth, scraping down the sides as needed, then pour into the cake pan and smooth the top. Bake for 20 minutes, then rotate the cake and bake for another 20 minutes. Lower the heat to 325°F (160°C) and bake for a final 8 minutes, then remove from the oven.

While the cake is baking, make the glaze. Put all the ingredients into a medium saucepan on medium heat and cook until the mixture bubbles and reduces to a syrup, 7–8 minutes. While still warm from the oven, poke holes in the surface of the cake, then pour the glaze over evenly. Leave to cool completely.

Put all the chocolate topping ingredients into a bowl and whisk until smooth.

Once the cake has cooled, remove from the pan, spread some of the chocolate topping over evenly and serve.

Transfer the remaining chocolate topping to an airtight jar and store it in the fridge for up to 2 weeks. Use it as a spread for toast or pancakes, or spoon over yogurt or ice cream.

Passion fruit & white chocolate mousse with cacao-cinnamon crumbs

White chocolate mousse is a classic dessert often found at kilo restaurants—casual, self-service spots where food is sold by weight, letting diners create their own perfect plate. I love the freedom of choosing my own adventure at kilos, and my favorite is Broth, on Avenida Rainha Elizabeth da Bélgica in Ipanema, Rio.

This white chocolate mousse is infused with passion fruit for a tangy twist and served with a bitter spiced cocoa crumble to cut through the sweetness.

Serves 6	V
Prep time: 10–15 minutes	
Cook time: 20 minutes	
Rest time: 4 hours plus overnight	

4 large eggs, separated

1⅓ cups (300 g) heavy cream

½ tsp vanilla bean paste

10½ oz (300 g) good-quality white chocolate, finely chopped

⅓ cup (60 g) passion fruit purée (or the strained pulp from 5–6 passion fruits)

zest of 2 tangerines

½ tsp chile flakes

¼ tsp ground cinnamon

⅛ tsp fine sea salt

1 tbsp cocoa powder (100% cocoa solids), to dust

Crumbs

¼ cup (60 g) coconut oil

6½ oz (180 g) ginger snap cookies, roughly broken

2 oz (60 g) dark chocolate, broken into chunks

⅓ cup (30 g) cocoa powder (100% cocoa solids)

¾ tsp ground cinnamon

¼ tsp fine salt

Put the yolks into a large heatproof bowl with the cream and vanilla. Set the bowl over a pan of very gently simmering water on low heat. Cook for about 15 minutes, stirring constantly until thickened to a pouring custard consistency. If the eggs start to scramble at all, remove from the heat for a minute to lower the temperature.

Remove from the heat and add the chopped white chocolate to the warm custard. Let it sit for 5 minutes, then gently stir until the chocolate is fully incorporated and the mixture is smooth. Add the passion fruit, tangerine zest, chile flakes, cinnamon and fine salt. Gently mix to combine, but don't overmix. Cover and refrigerate for at least 4 hours, or until completely chilled.

After 4 hours or once very well chilled and set, whip the egg whites. Put them into the bowl of a stand mixer with the whisk attachment in place, and whip on a medium–high speed to get stiff peaks, about 2 minutes.

Add a spoonful of the egg whites to the cooled custard and gently stir until incorporated. Fold in the remainder of the egg whites in stages until just incorporated—don't overmix or you'll knock out the air. Transfer to an 8½-cup (2-liter) container and dust the surface liberally with cocoa powder. Refrigerate overnight.

For the crumbs, gently melt the coconut oil and let it cool. Put it into a food processor with the rest of the crumb ingredients and pulse to get a finely chopped mixture. Make sure you don't over-process—you want small chunks of cookie and dark chocolate, not a powder. Tip into a container and refrigerate until cool and hardened. Once hard, break up into small chunks again.

Serve the mousse with the crumbs on top.

Note
If you don't have a food processor, put the cookies into a bag and bash with a rolling pin to get fine crumbs. Very finely chop the chocolate, then mix all the crumbs ingredients together.

Corn cake with guava-strawberry jam, cinnamon cream & caramelized coconut

Corn, guava and coconut are some of my favorite quintessentially Brazilian ingredients and I'm powerless before the combination of all three. This cake is moist from all the fresh corn—rather than spongy—and it comes together very easily in a blender or food processor.

For the jam I've used guava juice, because it's nearly impossible to get ripe guava where I live. The papaya jam (page 27) also works beautifully here. All the toppings—the jam, cream and caramelized coconut—can be made up to 3 days before if you want to get ahead. You can also skip the toppings and serve the cake warm with butter and store-bought jam.

Serves 6 V
Prep time: 10 minutes
Cook time: 56–58 minutes
Cool time: 2 hours

Cake

8 tbsp (120 g) ghee (from a jar, not a can; or use butter)
4 large eggs
1⅔ cups (280 g) canned corn kernels (drained weight)
2⅓ cup (200 g) unsweetened shredded coconut
¾ cup (140 g) light brown sugar
zest of 2 tangerines
zest of 1 lime
1 tsp baking powder
1 tsp vanilla bean paste
1 tsp ground cinnamon
½ tsp ground ginger
¼ tsp fine sea salt

Guava–strawberry jam

1 lb (500 g) ripe strawberries, stalks removed and roughly chopped
1⅔ cups (400 g) guava juice (one with as little sugar as possible)
2 tsp honey (or maple/agave syrup)
1 lime, halved

Caramelized coconut flakes

1⅔ cups (100 g) coconut flakes
⅓ cup (100 g) maple syrup
a good pinch of sea salt flakes

Preheat the oven to 375°F (190°C). Line and lightly grease an 8 in (20 cm) cake pan. Line a baking sheet with parchment paper.

First melt the ghee, then leave to cool for a few minutes. Put the cooled, melted ghee into a food processor or blender, along with all the remaining cake ingredients. Blend until smooth, scraping down the sides as needed.

Spoon the batter into the prepared cake pan and smooth out the top. Bake for 35 minutes, then lower the oven temperature to 350°F (180°C). Rotate the pan and bake for another 10 minutes, or until a skewer or knife comes out clean. Remove from the oven and set aside to cool.

Put the coconut flakes, maple syrup and salt into a bowl and mix so the flakes are thoroughly coated in the syrup. Spread out on the lined baking sheet. Bake for 7 minutes, mix well, then bake for another 8–10 minutes, or until crisp, caramelized and well browned. Set aside to cool.

For the jam, put all the ingredients into a 10 in (25 cm) wide pot and place on high heat. Bring to a rolling simmer and cook, stirring often, until reduced to a loose jam consistency, 20–30 minutes. Set aside to cool.

Put the mascarpone, yogurt, maple syrup, vanilla and cinnamon into a medium bowl and use a hand whisk to whip them together until thickened—this will take a few minutes and some muscle.

Once the cake has cooled completely (this is important, otherwise the cream will melt), top with the cream. Spoon some of the jam (you won't need it all) into the center and swirl it through.

Arrange the coconut flakes around the edge. Serve with more jam on the side.

Cinnamon cream

scant 1 cup (200 g) mascarpone (or heavy cream)
⅓ cup (80 g) Greek yogurt
2½ tbsp maple syrup
1 tsp vanilla bean paste
½ tsp ground cinnamon

Bolo de macaxeira, coco e maracuja

My mom loves the combination of cassava (or *macaxeira*, as it's known in the north-east of Brazil), coconut and passion fruit, so I always make this cake for her birthday. I adore the unique texture of baked cassava: it's caramelized and crispy on the outside and chewy on the inside, sort of like a cross between kouign-amann and mochi. As with most of my desserts, it's not overly sweet, which makes it the perfect mid-morning or afternoon treat with coffee.

The only time-consuming part of this recipe is peeling, grating and squeezing the cassava, after which all the ingredients come together very simply in a bowl. I often use frozen grated cassava (available online and in many Asian supermarkets), which makes the process a lot quicker.

Serves 8 — GF, V

Prep time: 10 minutes
Cook time: 1 hour
Cool time: 30 minutes

- 1 lb 3 oz (1 kg) cassava root (or 1 lb/500 g store-bought frozen grated cassava, defrosted)
- 8 passion fruits (or ⅓ cup/90 g passion fruit purée)
- 6 tbsp (80 g) unsalted butter, plus extra for greasing
- 3 tbsp demerara or coarse brown sugar
- ⅔ cup (150 g) light brown sugar
- 1 × 14 oz (400 g) can full-fat coconut milk
- ⅔ cup (50 g) unsweetened shredded coconut
- 1 egg, whisked
- 2 tsp tangerine or orange zest (from 2 tangerines)
- 1½ tsp lime zest (from 2 limes)
- 1 tsp vanilla bean paste
- ¼ tsp ground cinnamon
- ¼ tsp fine salt

Preheat the oven to 410°F (210°C).

Prep the cassava (see page 21; make sure to remove the hard stringy center).

Finely grate the cassava using the smaller holes of a box grater—you should get around 1 lb 9 oz (700 g). Transfer the grated cassava to a colander and place in the sink. Squeeze the grated cassava vigorously with your hands to get rid of as much liquid as possible—you should end up with 1 lb (500 g). Transfer to a large bowl.

Halve the passion fruits and scoop the flesh into a sieve set over the bowl of grated cassava. Push down on the flesh with a spoon to extract all the liquid. Discard the seeds.

Grease an 8 in (20 cm) nonstick cake pan with butter, then line the bottom with a circle of parchment paper. Put 1 tablespoon of the demerara or coarse brown sugar into the pan and shake to cover the buttery sides.

Melt the 6 tbsp (80 g) of butter over medium heat until beginning to brown and smell caramelized, about 6 minutes. Cool for a few minutes.

Add the browned butter, the light brown sugar, coconut milk, shredded coconut, egg, tangerine zest, lime zest, vanilla, cinnamon and ¼ teaspoon of fine salt to the bowl of grated cassava. Mix until thoroughly combined.

Spoon into the pan, level the surface, then sprinkle the remaining 2 tablespoons of demerara or coarse brown sugar evenly over to cover. Bake for 1 hour, or until the top is crisp and golden brown. Leave to cool completely, then run a knife around the edge of the cake to release it from the tin—this might be a little tricky, as the sugar will have hardened.

Place a rack over the pan, then flip the cake onto the rack. Remove the parchment, then carefully flip the cake back over so the crunchy, sugary side is on top. Use a sharp serrated knife to slice and enjoy with coffee.

See page 252 for a recipe photo. →

Chocolate ganache

Somewhere between a ganache and a mousse, this recipe is *extremely* easy and even more versatile. I guarantee it will become a go-to dessert when you need something delicious, quickly. What's more, it's vegan!

You can use it as a cake ganache (on the chocolate torte opposite, for example) or build it into a dessert, layering it with whipped cream, yogurt or crème fraîche, macerated fruit (ripe fruit + citrus juice + sugar/honey/maple syrup) and spiced caramelized nuts (page 239).

This recipe uses coconut yogurt, which is slightly sweet and not too acidic. If you don't need it to be vegan, I would suggest using ¾ cup (180 g) of plain yogurt and 5 tbsp (70 g) of heavy cream, as regular dairy yogurt is much more acidic and doesn't really work by itself in this context.

Prep time: 5 minutes	GF, V, VG
Cook time: 3–4 minutes	
Cool time: 5 minutes	

- 7 oz (200 g) dark chocolate (check it's vegan), broken into pieces
- 1 cup (250 g) coconut yogurt, fridge cold
- ¼ cup (80 g) maple syrup
- 2 tbsp runny tahini (mix well before measuring, to combine solid and fat)
- ½ tsp fine sea salt
- 1 tsp vanilla bean paste
- ½ tsp ground cinnamon
- zest of 1 tangerine

Bring a saucepan of water to a simmer. Place the chocolate in a clean dry bowl and place over the pan to melt. Once nearly melted, remove the bowl from the pan. Gently stir to finish melting the rest of the chocolate, then leave to cool for 5 minutes, so it's just warm but not piping hot.

Meanwhile, put all the remaining ingredients into a separate large bowl. Spoon in the melted chocolate and gently fold everything together until you get a texture somewhere between a mousse and a ganache; the mixture will start off quite loose but will thicken and aerate as you fold it, this should only take 20–30 seconds. Don't overmix or it will thicken too much.

Use as a cake ganache or layer into a dessert (see intro).

See pages 266 and 267 for a recipe photo. →

Spiced chocolate torte

This torte is crispy on the outside, with a rich, ganache-like center. The list of ingredients may look a little virtuous—the addition of beets and avocado making it *almost* healthy, but I promise you it's incredibly delicious.

As it is, the torte is vegan, dairy-free, gluten-free, grain-free and refined-sugar-free (as long as you leave out the sugar topping)—however, I like to serve it with sheep's yogurt, crème fraîche or heavy cream.

It's important that you let the torte cool and set before you remove it from the tin. Let it cool for 1–2 hours and you'll have a ganache-like interior, let it set overnight and it will turn into a fudgy brownie texture—both versions are wonderful.

Serves 6   GF, V, VG
Prep time: 5 minutes
Cook time: 40–45 minutes
Cool time: 2 hours

Cake batter

9 oz (250 g) plain cooked beets, drained (I use store-bought—make sure they're not in vinegar!)
7 oz (200 g) dark chocolate, roughly chopped
⅔ cup (200 g) maple syrup, plus extra to serve
1 ripe avocado, peeled and pitted (5 oz/140 g)
¾ cup (100 g) whole pecans or almonds
¾ cup (60 g) cocoa powder (100% cocoa solids)
zest of 1 tangerine or orange
1 tsp instant coffee (or use regular ground coffee)
1 tsp vanilla bean paste
¾ tsp ground cinnamon
¼ tsp chile flakes (regular or smoked)
¼ tsp fine sea salt

Topping

3 tbsp maple syrup
2 tbsp light brown sugar
sea salt flakes

To serve

crème fraîche, coconut or sheep's yogurt or heavy cream

Preheat the oven to 410°F (210°C). Line an 8 in (20 cm) cake pan with parchment paper.

Put all the batter ingredients into a food processor or blender and blend until smooth, scraping down the sides as needed.

Spoon into the prepared pan and level out the top. Drizzle over the maple syrup, sprinkle over the brown sugar, then swirl into the surface with a spoon. Sprinkle ½ teaspoon of sea salt flakes evenly over.

Bake for 40–45 minutes, or until crisp on top. The cake will still be quite soft inside, but this is what you want. Leave to cool in the pan for 2 hours before serving—this is important, so the cake can set.

Serve with crème fraîche, sheep's yogurt or heavy cream, with a little extra maple syrup and sea salt flakes on top.

See pages 266 and 267 for a recipe photo. →

Maple caramel & cinnamon-coffee cream pavê

Pavê (pah-vey) is made by layering cream with cookies and flavors like chocolate, caramel, peanut, guava or banana. It's sort of similar in structure to tiramisu, which my version is also inspired by. This is a showstopper, perfect for birthdays or special occasions. The chocolate shards really add a glamorous touch, so don't skip them. Although the recipe looks long, it's straightforward, with no technical steps—just remember to let it set overnight. If you want to get ahead, it keeps well in the fridge for up to 3 days before serving. You'll need 2⅔ cups (600 g) heavy cream, 10½ oz (300 g) dark chocolate and ¾ cup (220 g) maple syrup in total for the recipe.

Serves 6   V
Prep time: 15–20 minutes
Cook time: 15–20 minutes
Rest time: overnight plus 2 hours

Chocolate ganache

scant 1 cup (200 g) heavy cream
5¼ oz (150 g) dark chocolate
a good pinch of sea salt flakes

Miso caramel

½ cup (140 g) maple syrup
5 tbsp (70 g) heavy cream
1½ tbsp white miso paste
1 tsp vanilla bean paste

Cinnamon-coffee cream

2¼ cups (500 g) full-fat mascarpone
1½ cups (330 g) heavy cream
¼ cup (80 g) maple syrup
1¼ tbsp ground coffee
1 tbsp tangerine or orange zest (from 3 tangerines)
2 tsp ground cinnamon
1½ tsp vanilla bean paste
½ tsp sea salt flakes

Coffee-soaked cookies

4 tbsp instant coffee powder
1¼ cups (300 g) boiling water
2 tbsp mezcal (or other spirit of your choice; optional)
10½ oz (300 g) savoiardi cookies (aka lady fingers)

To finish

5¼ oz (150 g) dark chocolate
1 tbsp cocoa powder (100% cocoa solids)

See pages 270 and 271 for a recipe photo. →

For the ganache, put the cream, chocolate and sea salt flakes into a heatproof bowl and place on top of a small pot of gently simmering water. Heat until the chocolate starts to melt, then turn off the heat and leave for 5 minutes. Stir gently to incorporate the chocolate, but don't overmix.

For the miso caramel, put all the ingredients into a medium pot and place on medium heat. Cook for about 7–10 minutes, whisking continuously; the mixture should bubble away and thicken to the consistency of a pourable caramel sauce. Transfer to a bowl and set aside until completely cool.

For the cinnamon-coffee cream, put the mascarpone into a large bowl. Slowly add the heavy cream, using a hand whisk to mix until smooth and combined. Add the rest of the ingredients and whisk to incorporate—don't overmix.

For the coffee-soaked cookies, put the instant coffee into a heatproof container, add the boiling water (or brew 1¼ cups/ 300 g of extremely strong coffee), and stir to combine. Add the mezcal or another booze of your choice, if you like.

Line a 10 in (25 cm) square cake pan with two layers of plastic wrap. Spoon half of the cream into the pan and smooth the surface with the back of a spoon. Spoon over half each of the cooled melted chocolate and cooled caramel and swirl together.

Add the cookies to the coffee two at a time and soak for about 2 seconds on each side. Don't over-soak or they'll become soggy.

Form a layer of soaked cookies on top of the caramel and chocolate. Repeat these layers—cream, caramel, chocolate ganache, coffee-soaked cookies—once more. Cover with plastic wrap and chill overnight, or for up to 3 days.

Melt the chocolate for the shards in a bowl set over a pan of gently simmering water.

Prepare a large sheet of parchment paper on a flat tray that will fit into your fridge. Pour the melted chocolate onto the paper and quickly spread it out into a thin layer using a spatula. Refrigerate until completely cool and set, about 2 hours.

Place a large platter on top of the cake pan, then carefully flip the pan and platter over. Remove the pan and gently peel the plastic wrap off the cake. Break the chocolate into shards, then stud them onto the cake. Slice and serve.

Chico tropical with coconut custard & honey meringue

I've named this layered dessert *Chico tropical* (shee-koo tro-pee-kow) as a nod to the classic *Chico balanceado*, which is a caramelized banana, custard and meringue pudding. The original is said to be inspired by Chico Da Silva, a 1940s figure known for charming his way out of trouble. The *"balanceado"* refers to the dessert's supposed perfect balance (although I've always found it far too sweet and creamy).

In my version I swap the caramelized bananas for fresh papaya, mango and passion fruit. I use maple syrup and coconut milk in the custard instead of condensed milk and I replace sugar in the meringue with honey. The result is what I truly believe to be the *perfect balance* (i.e. not too sweet and a little sour from the fruit).

For an English-style trifle twist, add a sponge finger layer to the bottom of the dessert, in which case you won't need to remove the juice in step 6 because it will soak into the cookies.

If you don't have a blowtorch to brown the meringue, build the dessert in an ovenproof dish and briefly brown it under a very hot broiler.

Serves 6 GF, V
Prep time: 15–20 minutes
Cook time: 20–22 minutes
Chilleng time: overnight

Fruit layer

- 7 oz (200 g) ripe peeled papaya, cut into ¾ in (2 cm) pieces
- 7 oz (200 g) ripe peeled mango, cut into ¾ in (2 cm) pieces
- scant ½ cup (80 g) passion fruit pulp and seeds (around 5 passion fruits depending on size)
- 1 tbsp honey (or maple/agave syrup)
- zest of 1 lime

Coconut custard

- 1 × 14 oz (400 g) can of full-fat coconut milk
- 5 egg yolks (save 3 of the whites for the meringue)
- 4 tbsp maple syrup
- 1 tbsp cornstarch
- 1 tsp vanilla bean paste
- ⅛ tsp fine sea salt

Honey meringue topping

- ⅓ cup (100 g) honey (or maple/agave syrup)
- 3 egg whites
- 1½ tsp rice vinegar
- 1 tsp vanilla bean paste
- ½ tsp ground cinnamon
- ⅛ tsp fine sea salt

Put all the fruit layer ingredients into a large bowl and gently mix to combine, taking care not to crush the fruit. Set aside.

For the custard, bring a medium saucepan of water to a simmer over low heat.

Place all the custard ingredients in a clean, dry bowl (make sure to set aside 3 of the egg whites in a separate clean, dry container, for the meringue; you can store these in the fridge overnight, just let them come to room temperature before making meringue).

Whisk the custard ingredients together until completely smooth. Place the bowl over the saucepan of simmering water and gently cook, whisking continuously. Make sure to cook the custard slowly over low heat, to avoid scrambling the yolks. You're looking for a thick but pourable consistency, which should take 20–22 minutes. Pass the custard through a sieve to get rid of any lumps, then whisk well to recombine. Set aside at room temp until cool.

Drain the fruit to remove most of the juice (otherwise the bottom layer will be soggy), then transfer the fruit to a 9 in (22 cm) glass serving bowl. Spoon the custard over to create an even layer. Cover with plastic wrap and refrigerate overnight, until set.

Make the meringue up to 3 hours before serving. Put all the ingredients into the bowl of a stand mixer and mix—just to combine the honey and eggs. With the whisk attachment in place, whip on medium–high speed for about 3½ minutes, or until you get stiff, shiny peaks.

Spoon the meringue onto the custard layer, creating dips and peaks with the back of a spoon. Use a blowtorch to evenly burn the meringue, and serve straight away.

Note
You'll need to start a day ahead, so the custard layer sets properly.

Basil & clove limonada

This incredibly refreshing drink is inspired by the wonderful Heloísa (see page 45). She makes a version with *folhas de cravo da Índia* (clove leaves) which she grows in her *horta*. For the lack of clove leaves, I'm using a combination of basil and cloves, which results in a similar flavor. I've sweetened my version with honey instead of sugar, and I also add a bit of green chile for an extra kick. The spinach leaves just help keep the drink greener for longer.

Serves 4   GF, V, VG
Prep time: 5 minutes

2 whole limes
2 whole lemons
⅓ cup (100 g) honey (or maple/agave syrup)
1¾ oz (50 g) basil leaves
½ oz (15 g) spinach leaves
4 whole cloves
½ a green bird's-eye chile (or less/more if you like)
3½ cups (800 g) still water

Remove the tops and bottoms of the limes and lemons, then slice or peel away the skin and pith with a sharp knife. Put them into the blender whole (don't worry about removing the seeds) along with all the other ingredients.

Blend very well, then strain through a sieve, pushing down on the pulp to extract all the flavor.

Serve at once, over plenty of ice.

Guava, strawberry & black pepper caipirinha

Try and get pure guava puree or juice for this, or one with no added flavorings and little added sugar.

Serves 4   GF, V, VGO
Prep time: 3 minutes

¾ cup (200 g) guava juice or purée
⅔ cup (160 g) tangerine juice (4–6 tangerines)
½ cup (120 g) cachaça or mezcal
⅓ cup (100 g) honey (or maple/agave syrup) (or more, to taste)
3 oz (80 g) strawberries, tops removed
¼ cup (60 g) lemon juice (2–3 lemons)
2 tbsp lime juice (1–2 limes), plus extra to serve
60 drops of Angostura bitters
30 twists of freshly cracked pepper (⅛ tsp)
1 cinnamon stick, roughly broken

Put all the ingredients into a blender and blend well.

Strain, pushing down on the strawberry and cinnamon bits to extract flavor. Serve over ice with a squeeze of fresh lime and some freshly cracked pepper on top.

Spiced rooibos & tangerine mate

This is my take on the classic mate (mah-chee), a traditional South American tea made from yerba mate leaves. In Brazil, mate is famously associated with the *Matte Leão* brand, known for its distinctive double "t."

This version blends the floral, honeyed notes of rooibos—a tea from South Africa that I love—with zingy citrus and warming spices. Serve ice cold!

Serves 6 GF, V, VGO
Prep time: 3 minutes
Rest time: 15 minutes, plus overnight

- 4 rooibos tea bags
- 3 yerba maté tea bags (or use black tea)
- scant ½ cup (100 g) tangerine juice (3–4 tangerines), plus extra to serve
- 3 tbsp lime juice (2 small limes), plus extra to serve
- ⅓ cup (80 g) honey (or maple/agave syrup)
- 3 cinnamon sticks
- 1 tsp vanilla bean paste
- 15 drops of Angostura bitters
- 2 cups (500 g) boiling water
- mezcal, to serve

Put all the iced tea ingredients into a heatproof jug/container and stir well. Leave to infuse for 15 minutes, then top up with another 1½ cups (350 g) of cold water.

Leave to infuse overnight, for the flavors to develop.

Strain, then serve over ice with a splash of mezcal and some more fresh lime and tangerine.

INDEX

A

Amazon rainforest 108–5, 194, 197
angu with roasted oyster mushroom & spiced tomato sauce 35
Asiedu, Joshua Kwaku 124–5
avocados: chilled avocado soup 82
azeite de dendê 20, 124–33
    papaya & *dendê* dip 68
    spatchcock chicken with *dendê* & coconut peppercorn sauce 214

B

bacon: chicken, bacon & scallion skewers with stroganoff sauce 206
bake, *picadinho* & sweet potato 220
banana ice cream, roasted 239
banana leaves 21
    corn & coconut *pamonha* in banana leaf 56
    crab *pamonha* in banana leaves 107
basil: basil & clove *limonada* 274
    stir-fried papaya with crispy basil 48
batata palha 31
    tuna tartare with red pepper *pimenta* & *batata palha* 146
beef: green pancakes with yogurt sauce 209–10
    picadinho & sweet potato bake 220
    picanha with charred chile, garlic & lime butter 228–9
    quick steaks with coffee & chile butter 230
    vaca atolada 205
beets: chicken in beet sauce 190
black-eyed pea cakes with toasted coconut salsa 98
black turtle beans 20
    feijão with chocolate & spices 88
bolo de macaxeira, coco e maracuja 262
brioche burger buns: *moqueca* fish burgers 120
broths: ginger, tomato & lime broth 122
    golden tomato broth 200
    spicy tomato broth 186
Buarque, Chico 84, 87
burgers, *moqueca* fish 120
butter 22
    charred chile, garlic & lime butter 228–9
    chicken livers with *urucum*, paprika & coffee butter 222
    chile honey butter 91
    coffee & chile butter 230
    lime butter 143
    mango curry butter 150
    scallion butter 82
butternut squash, coconutty saffron orzo with roasted 55

C

cabbage: slaw 120
cacao-cinnamon crumbs 258
cachaça 20
    papaya, lime & chile granita 238
    caipirinha, guava, strawberry & black pepper 274
cakes: *bolo de macaxeira, coco e maracuja* 262
    corn cake with guava-strawberry jam, cinnamon cream & caramelized coconut 260
    papaya & chocolate cake 256
    pineapple torte 253
    spiced chocolate torte 265
Calabrians 224
camarão na moranga 154
caramel: caramelized coconut flakes 260
    maple caramel & cinnamon-coffee cream *pavê* 269
    spiced caramelized nuts 239
caranguejos 171
carrots: sweet & sour carrots with hot sauce & lime 79
Casa do Benin 164
cashew coconut chile oil 26
cassava 20, 21, 194–9
    bolo de macaxeira, coco e maracuja 262
    cassava, shrimp & onion fritters 174
    coconut & cassava fried fish 162
    main event *pirão* 169–70
    toasted cassava 182
    tuna & cassava in a ginger, tomato & lime broth 122
    vaca atolada 205
cauliflower purée 139
chard leaves: egg, tomato & greens soup 96
charutos with spicy tomato broth & garlic oil 186
cheese: corn pie with caramelized onions & green chile oil 100
    feta yogurt 91
    guava & cheese *pastéis* 250
chicken: chicken, bacon & scallion skewers with stroganoff sauce 206
    chicken in beet sauce 190
    coconut chicken with charred okra 180
    mango and *urucum* chicken 192
    spatchcock chicken with *dendê* & coconut peppercorn sauce 214
chicken livers with *urucum*, paprika & coffee butter 222
chickpea flour: plantain fritters 247
chico tropical with coconut custard & honey meringue 272
chiles 22
    cashew coconut chile oil 26
    chile ginger-garlic oil 80
    chile-ginger *tempero* 30
    chile honey butter 91
    chopped red chile condiment 29
    green chile oil 100
    green chile vinagrete 143, 169–70
    guava, curry & chile meatballs 226
    orange & burnt chile vinagrete 156
    papaya, lime & chile granita 238
    picanha with charred chile, garlic & lime butter 228–9
    quick steaks with coffee & chile butter 230
    roasted root vegetables with maple, lime & chile 90
    stir-fried watercress with garlic & chile 71
    tomato chile paste 169–70
    yellow chile mash 31

chocolate: chocolate fudge sauce 239
　　chocolate ganache 264, 269
　　feijão with chocolate & spices 88
　　papaya & chocolate cake with citrus honey glaze 256
　　passion fruit & white chocolate mousse with cacao-cinnamon crumbs 258
　　spiced chocolate torte 265
　　warm chocolate fudge sauce 247
　　cinnamon: cacao-cinnamon crumbs 258
　　cinnamon cream 260
　　cinnamon sugar 247
　　guava, cinnamon, strawberry & lime sorbet 234
　　maple caramel & cinnamon-coffee cream *pavê* 269
cilantro: cilantro & lime vinagrete 134
　　ginger-garlic-cilantro fries 70
citrus 60–101
　　citrus honey glaze 256
　　citrus pickled onions 27
clam *moqueca* with cilantro & lime vinagrete 134
cloves: basil & clove *limonada* 274
coconut: black-eyed pea cakes with toasted coconut salsa 98
　　caramelized coconut flakes 260
　　corn cake with guava-strawberry jam, cinnamon cream & caramelized coconut 260
coconut cream: roasted banana ice cream with chocolate fudge sauce 239
coconut milk 21
　　angu with roasted oyster mushroom & spiced tomato sauce 35
　　bolo de macaxeira, coco e maracuja 262
　　camarão na moranga 154
　　chico tropical with coconut custard & honey meringue 272
　　chilled avocado soup 82
　　clam *moqueca* with cilantro & lime vinagrete 134
　　coconut & cassava fried fish 162
　　coconut & ginger roasted cherry tomatoes 74
　　coconut chicken with charred okra 180
　　coconut rice pudding with guava-strawberry jam 244
　　coconutty saffron orzo with roasted squash 55
　　corn & coconut *pamonha* in banana leaf 56
　　corn pie with caramelized onions & green chile oil 100
　　crab, coconut & zucchini omelet 171
　　crab *pamonha* in banana leaves 107
　　curry sauce 214
　　escondidinho de peixe com couve flor 139
　　moqueca fish burgers 120
　　spatchcock chicken with *dendê* & coconut peppercorn sauce 214
　　warm chocolate fudge sauce 247
coconut oil: cashew coconut chile oil 26
coconut yogurt: chocolate ganache 264
　　lime yogurt 52
cod, flowers stuffed with shrimp & 116
coffee: chicken livers with *urucum*, paprika & coffee butter 222
　　maple caramel & cinnamon-coffee cream *pavê* 269
　　quick steaks with coffee & chile butter 230
comida da roça 40, 45
comida Mineira 40–1, 45, 46
Comunidade Ribeirinha Santo Antônio 194
condiment, chopped red chile 29
corn: corn & coconut *pamonha* in banana leaf 56
　　corn cake with guava-strawberry jam, cinnamon cream & caramelized coconut 260

corn pie with caramelized onions & green chile oil 100
crab *pamonha* in banana leaves 107
couve & blood orange salad 73
Cova da Onça 126–33
crab: crab, coconut & zucchini omelet 171
　　crab *pamonha* in banana leaves 107
cream: chocolate ganache 269
　　maple caramel & cinnamon-coffee cream *pavê* 269
　　passion fruit & white chocolate mousse 258
crudo: *crudo* with grated tomatoes & curried onions 105
　　scallop *crudo* 156
crumbs, cacao-cinnamon 258
Culinária Musical 164
curry: curried onions 105
　　curried red pepper ragout 56
　　curry sauce 214
　　guava, curry & chile meatballs 226
　　mango curry butter 150
custard, coconut 272

D

Dedé, Tia 240
dendê 12, 124–33
　　papaya & *dendê* dip 68
　　spatchcock chicken with *dendê* & coconut peppercorn sauce 214
Dona Rosa 194, 197
dressings: golden vinaigrette 29, 62
　　mango dressing 38
drinks: basil & clove *limonada* 274
　　guava, strawberry & black pepper *caipirinha* 274
　　spiced rooibos & tangerine mate 275
duck: duck in golden tomato broth 200
　　duck rice 217–18

E

eggs: chico tropical with coconut custard & honey meringue 272
　　crab, coconut & zucchini omelet 171
　　egg, tomato & greens soup 96
eggplants: roasted eggplant with mango sauce, lime yogurt & sesame salt 52
　　spiced eggplant ragout 50
escondidinho de peixe com couve flor 139
Eugênia, Vovó 240

F

farinha de mandioca 20, 194
　　coconut & cassava fried fish 162
　　toasted cassava 182
feijão 11
　　feijão with chocolate & spices 88
Feira de São Joaquim 164
fish 111
　　coconut & cassava fried fish 162
　　crudo with grated tomatoes & curried onions 105
　　escondidinho de peixe com couve flor 139
　　flowers stuffed with shrimp & cod 116
　　grilled fish with mango curry butter 150
　　main event *pirão* 169–70

Index

moqueca fish burgers 120
pastéis de forno with crunchy flaky spelt pastry 175
roast mackerel with lime butter & green chile vinagrete 143
tuna & cassava in a ginger, tomato & lime broth 122
tuna tartare with red pepper *pimenta* & *batata palha* 146
whole roasted plaice 134
flavor bombs 24–31
flowers stuffed with shrimp & cod 116
fries, ginger-garlic-cilantro 70
fritters: cassava, shrimp & onion fritters 174
 plantain fritters with warm chocolate fudge sauce 247
fruit, citrus 60–101
fudge sauces, chocolate 239, 247

G

ganache, chocolate 264, 269
garlic: charred chile, garlic & lime butter 228–9
 chile ginger-garlic oil 80
 garlic oil 186
 garlic yogurt 38
 ginger-garlic-cilantro fries 70
 ginger-garlic mix 26
 stir-fried watercress with garlic & chile 71
 tempero verde 28
ginger: chile ginger-garlic oil 80
 chile-ginger *tempero* 30
 coconut & ginger roasted cherry tomatoes 74
 ginger-garlic-cilantro fries 70
 ginger-garlic mix 26
 mango, ginger & lemon sorbet 234
 tempero verde 28
 tuna & cassava in a ginger, tomato & lime broth 122
gnocchi, sweet potato 50
golden tomato broth 200
golden vinaigrette 29, 62
granita, papaya, lime & chile 238
greens: egg, tomato & greens soup 96
 fried greens with charred red pepper pimento 94
 green pancakes with yogurt sauce 209–10
 green vinagrete 202
guava 21
 guava & cheese *pastéis* 250
 guava, cinnamon, strawberry & lime sorbet 234
 guava jam: guava, curry & chile meatballs 226
 guava strawberry jam 244, 250, 260
 guava juice: guava, strawberry & black pepper *caipirinha* 274
 guava-strawberry jam 244, 250, 260

H

Heloísa 13, 45–6, 60, 274
herbs: *tempero verde* 28
honey: chile honey butter 91
 citrus honey glaze 256
 honey meringue 272
hot sauce: sweet & sour carrots with hot sauce & lime 79

I

ice cream, roasted banana 239
immigration 12, 184, 212, 224
ingredients 20–3
Iracema, Vovó 240
Italian immigration 12, 13, 224

J

Jacira, Tia 240
jam: guava strawberry jam 244, 250, 260
 papaya or mango jam 27
Japanese immigration 12, 13, 212

K

kabocha squash: *camarão na moranga* 154

L

Lacruz, Kenrick (Papa Kenrick) 13, 108–15
lamb: *charutos* with spicy tomato broth & garlic oil 186
 lamb with pineapple *pimenta* & toasted cassava 182
Lebanese 12, 184
leeks with golden vinaigrette 62
lemons 60
 basil & clove *limonada* 274
 mango, ginger & lemon sorbet 234
Levantine cuisine 184
Liberdade, São Paulo 212
limão cravo 21, 60
limes 60
 basil & clove *limonada* 274
 charred chile, garlic & lime butter 228–9
 cilantro & lime vinagrete 134
 guava, cinnamon, strawberry & lime sorbet 234
 lime butter 143
 lime yogurt 52
 papaya, lime & chile granita 238
 roasted root vegetables with maple, lime & chile 90
 sweet & sour carrots with hot sauce & lime 79
 tuna & cassava in a ginger, tomato & lime broth 122
limonada, basil & clove 274

M

macaxeira 21, 194–9
 bolo de macaxeira, coco e maracuja 262
mackerel: roast mackerel with lime butter & green chile vinagrete 143
main event *pirão* 169–70
Manaus 108–9, 212
mango jam 27
 mango curry butter 150
mango juice: mango and *urucum* chicken 192
 mango dressing 38
 shrimp, okra & mango juice stew 148
mangoes 22
 chico tropical with coconut custard & honey meringue 272

mango and *urucum* chicken 192
mango, ginger & lemon sorbet 234
roasted eggplant with mango sauce, lime yogurt
 & sesame salt 52
tomato, mango & pickled onion salad 63
manioc 194–9
maple syrup: maple caramel & cinnamon-coffee
 cream *pavê* 269
roasted root vegetables with maple, lime & chile 90
mascarpone: cinnamon-coffee cream 269
cinnamon cream 260
mate, spiced rooibos & tangerine 275
maxixada 164
maxixe 22, 164
meat 178–81
meatballs, guava, curry & chile 226
meringue, honey 272
mezcal: guava, strawberry & black pepper *caipirinha* 274
papaya, lime & chile granita 238
Middle Eastern immigration 184
Minas Gerais 40–1, 180, 190, 205
miso caramel 269
moqueca 12
clam *moqueca* with cilantro & lime vinagrete 134
moqueca fish burgers 120
mousse, passion fruit & white chocolate 258
mushrooms: *angu* with roasted oyster mushroom
 & spiced tomato sauce 35
music 84–7

N

Nikkei 212
nuts, spiced caramelized 239

O

oils: cashew coconut chile oil 26
chile ginger-garlic oil 80
garlic oil 186
green chile oil 100
shrimp oil 116
okra 22
coconut chicken with charred okra 180
fried greens with charred
 red pepper pimento 94
okra skewers with mango dressing 38
shrimp, okra & mango juice stew 148
omelet, crab, coconut & zucchini 171
onions: cassava, shrimp & onion fritters 174
citrus pickled onions 27
corn pie with caramelized onions
 & green chile oil 100
curried onions 105
tomato, mango & pickled onion salad 63
ora-pro-nóbis 40–1
oranges: blood oranges with chile ginger-garlic oil 80
couve & blood orange salad 73
orange & burnt chile vinagrete 156
orzo: coconutty saffron orzo with roasted squash 55

P

Palestinians 12, 184
palm oil 12, 20, 124–33
papaya & *dendê* dip 68
spatchcock chicken with *dendê*
 & coconut peppercorn sauce 214
pamonha: corn & coconut *pamonha* in banana leaf 56
crab *pamonha* in banana leaves 107
pancakes: green pancakes with yogurt sauce 209–10
pancetta: guava, curry & chile meatballs 226
panquecas com molho branco 209–10
papaya 22
chico tropical with coconut custard & honey meringue 272
papaya & chocolate cake with citrus honey glaze 256
papaya & *dendê* dip 68
papaya jam 27
papaya, lime & chile granita 238
stir-fried papaya with crispy basil 48
paprika: chicken livers with *urucum*, paprika & coffee butter 222
passion fruit: *bolo de macaxeira, coco e maracuja* 262
chico tropical with coconut custard & honey meringue 272
passion fruit & white chocolate mousse 258
pasta: coconutty saffron orzo with roasted squash 55
pastéis: guava & cheese *pastéis* 250
pastéis de forno with crunchy flaky spelt pastry 175
pastry, crunchy spelt 175, 250
pavê, maple caramel & cinnamon-coffee cream 269
peppercorns: guava, strawberry & black pepper *caipirinha* 274
spatchcock chicken with *dendê* & coconut
 peppercorn sauce 214
peppers: charred red pepper *pimenta* 28
charred sweet & sour peppers 76
curried red pepper ragout 56
escondidinho de peixe com couve flor 139
fried greens with charred red pepper pimento 94
picadinho & sweet potato bake 220
red pepper *pimenta* 146
picadinho & sweet potato bake 220
picanha with charred chile, garlic & lime butter 228–9
pickles: pickled onions 27, 63
pickled shallots 158–9, 182
pie: corn pie with caramelized onions & green chile oil 100
pimenta 22
charred red pepper *pimenta* 28
pineapple *pimenta* 30
red pepper *pimenta* 146
pimento, fried greens with charred red pepper 94
pineapple: lamb with pineapple *pimenta* &
 toasted cassava 182
pineapple *pimenta* 30
pineapple torte 253
slow-cooked pineapple pork with green vinagrete 202
pineapple juice: mango sauce 52
slow-cooked pineapple pork with green vinagrete 202
pirão, main event 169–70
plaice: grilled fish with mango curry butter 150
whole roasted plaice 134
plantain 20
plantain fritters with warm chocolate fudge sauce 247
plantains with chile honey butter 91
tropical shrimp with plantain and pickled shallots 158–9

Index

polenta: *angu* with roasted oyster mushroom & spiced tomato sauce 35
    corn & coconut *pamonha* in banana leaf 56
    crab *pamonha* in banana leaves 107
politics 11, 84–7
pork: guava, curry & chile meatballs 226
    slow-cooked pineapple pork with green vinagrete 202
porridge: main event *pirão* 169–70
potatoes: *batata palha* 31
    ginger-garlic-cilantro fries 70

R

ragout: curried red pepper ragout 56
    spiced eggplant ragout 50
rainbow chard: *charutos* with spicy tomato broth & garlic oil 186
red mullet: *crudo* with grated tomatoes & curried onions 105
red palm oil 12, 20, 124–33
    papaya & *dendê* dip 68
    spatchcock chicken with *dendê* & coconut peppercorn sauce 214
rice: coconut rice pudding with guava-strawberry jam 244
    duck rice 217–18
ricotta: feta yogurt 91
    guava & cheese *pastéis* 250
Rio Negro 108, 109
rooibos: spiced rooibos & tangerine mate 275

S

saffron: coconutty saffron orzo 55
salads: *couve* & blood orange salad 73
    tomato, mango & pickled onion salad 63
salsas 98
    grated tomato salsa 171
salt, sesame 52
Salvador 164
samba 84
Sandoval, Vovô 240
São Paulo 212
sauces: chocolate fudge sauce 239
    curry sauce 214
    mango sauce 52
    moqueca sauce 120
    spiced tomato sauce 35
    warm chocolate fudge sauce 247
savoiardi cookies: coffee-soaked cookies 269
scallions: chicken, bacon & scallion skewers with stroganoff sauce 206
    scallion butter 82
scallop *crudo* with orange & burnt chile vinagrete 156
sea bream: *crudo* with grated tomatoes & curried onions 105
    main event *pirão* 169–70
seafood 102–77
sesame salt 52
shallots, pickled 158–9, 182
shrimp 20
    camarão na moranga 154
    cassava, shrimp & onion fritters 174
    escondidinho de peixe com couve flor 139
    flowers stuffed with shrimp & cod 116
    main event *pirão* 169–70
    shrimp, okra & mango juice stew 148
    tropical shrimp with plantain and pickled shallots 158–9
Sicilians 224
Silvio 13, 126–33
skewers, chicken, bacon & scallion 206
slaw 120
sorbet: guava, cinnamon, strawberry & lime sorbet 234
    mango, ginger & lemon sorbet 234
soups: chilled avocado soup 82
    egg, tomato & greens soup 96
spelt flour: crunchy spelt pastry 175, 250
    green pancakes with yogurt sauce 209–10
    pineapple torte 253
spiced eggplant ragout 50
spiced caramelized nuts 239
spiced chocolate torte 265
spiced rooibos & tangerine mate 275
spiced tomato sauce 35
spices, *feijão* with chocolate & 88
spinach: fried greens with charred red pepper pimento 94
    green pancakes with yogurt sauce 209–10
spring greens, *couve* & blood orange salad 73
squash: *camarão na moranga* 154
    coconutty saffron orzo with roasted squash 55
squash flowers stuffed with shrimp & cod 116
stews 12, 164
    clam *moqueca* with cilantro & lime vinagrete 134
    picadinho & sweet potato bake 220
    shrimp, okra & mango juice stew 148
    vaca atolada 205
strawberries: guava, cinnamon, strawberry & lime sorbet 234
    guava, strawberry & black pepper *caipirinha* 274
    guava strawberry jam 244, 250, 260
stroganoff sauce, chicken, bacon & scallion skewers with 206
sugar, cinnamon 247
sugar snap peas: *couve* & blood orange salad 73
sweet & sour carrots with hot sauce & lime 79
sweet potatoes: *picadinho* & sweet potato bake 220
    sweet potato gnocchi with spiced eggplant ragout 50
sweets 232–77
Swiss chard: *charutos* with spicy tomato broth & garlic oil 186
Syrians 12, 184

T

Tamimi, Sami 184
tangerine juice: guava, strawberry & black pepper *caipirinha* 274
    spiced rooibos & tangerine mate 275
tartare, tuna 146
tea: spiced rooibos & tangerine mate 275
tempero: chile-ginger *tempero* 30
    tempero verde 28, 190
Terminal Pesqueiro 108
tomatoes: *angu* with roasted oyster mushroom & spiced tomato sauce 35
    clam *moqueca* with cilantro & lime vinagrete 134
    coconut & ginger roasted cherry tomatoes 74
    coconut chicken with charred okra 180
    crudo with grated tomatoes & curried onions 105
    duck rice 217–18

egg, tomato & greens soup 96
golden tomato broth 200
golden vinaigrette 29, 62
grated tomato salsa 171
grated tomatoes 205, 209–10
lamb with pineapple *pimenta* & toasted cassava 182
moqueca fish burgers 120
orange & burnt chile vinagrete 156
pastéis de forno with crunchy flaky spelt pastry 175
salsa 98
spicy tomato broth 186
tomato chile paste 169–70
tomato, mango & pickled onion salad 63
tuna & cassava in a ginger, tomato & lime broth 122
vaca atolada 205
tortes: pineapple torte 253
    spiced chocolate torte 265
tropical shrimp with plantain and pickled shallots 158–9
tucupi 23, 194–9, 200
tuna: *pastéis de forno* with crunchy flaky spelt pastry 175
    tuna & cassava in a ginger, tomato & lime broth 122
    tuna tartare with red pepper *pimenta* & *batata palha* 146

U

umami paste 88, 209–10, 220
urucum 23
    chicken livers with *urucum*, paprika & coffee butter 222
    mango and *urucum* chicken 192

V

vaca atolada 205
vegetables 32–59
    roasted root vegetables with maple, lime & chile 90
vinagrete 23
    cilantro & lime vinagrete 134
    green chile vinagrete 143, 169–70
    green vinagrete 202
    orange & burnt chile vinagrete 156
vinaigrette, golden 29, 62
Vitorino, Vovó 240

W

Washington, Jorge 13, 164
watercress: stir-fried watercress with garlic & chile 71

Y

yerba maté tea: spiced rooibos & tangerine mate 275
yogurt: chocolate ganache 264
    cinnamon cream 260
    feta yogurt 91
    garlic yogurt 38
    green pancakes with yogurt sauce 209–10
    guava & cheese *pastéis* 250
    lime yogurt 52

Z

zucchini flowers stuffed with shrimp & cod 116
zucchinis: crab, coconut & zucchini omelet 171

THANKS

Endless thanks to my beautiful mãe, Maria Candida de Melo—my anchor and the inspiration for this book and to my darling Dad, Nicolas Belfrage, whose quiet wisdom and unwavering love I miss every single day. This book is for you both, with all my love.

Making a book is a team effort, and I've never felt that more deeply than with this one. So many extraordinary people brought their expertise and creativity to these pages and for that I am profoundly grateful.

Brazil

To my core teammates in Brazil: Romã Nesi Pio, Pedro Pinho and Warren Rodricks, thank you from the bottom of my heart. The three of you made those intense, crazy weeks of shooting some of the best of my life. The dawn starts and sleepless nights could have broken some, but we laughed through it all—I'll cherish those memories forever.

Romã, I am forever indebted to you for producing the shoot in Brazil, you absolute badass. The intricate planning, the security arrangements, the countless modes of transport—by land, water, air and everything in between—to places far off the beaten track. You made the impossible possible, over and over again.

Pedro, thank you for the breathtaking photographs of Brazil that bring this book to life. Your talent lies not only in what you beautifully capture, but in your gift for making everyone in front of your lens feel at ease. I'm convinced meeting you was fate, and I couldn't have asked for a better person to capture the heart and soul of this book.

Warren, what you've shot to promote this book is nothing short of a masterpiece. Thank you for managing to do it all on your own, for being everywhere at once, capturing jaw-dropping scenes and recording sound, all while finding your way in a new country without the language. Thank you to Shyam Patel for beautifully color-grading Warren's footage.

Thank you to Gabriela Cara and Bruna Cabeço for your tireless work helping Romã produce the shoot from afar, we couldn't have done it without you. Thank you to Tatiana Fernandes for an incredible couple of days cooking together in Rio and to Mateus Queiroz for helping us. Thank you to Bia Falcão for lending us all your beautiful props. Thank you to Nathalia Atayde Henrique, Felipe Santos da Costa and Gabi Dracxler for assisting on the shoot in Rio.

My deepest thanks to the contributors who have enriched this book.

In the Amazon, part 1: Kenrick Lacruz—our dear Papa Kenrick—thank you for the most unforgettable insight into your life in the jungle and for looking after us. Thank you to your beautiful family Roziane, Cloves, Kenrick Jr. and Natasha and to Diego, Marinauva, Rocigleice and Acassio for the hospitality and the delicious food.

In the Amazon, part 2: Thank you to Antonio Barroso, Antônia Monteiro and Clotildo Monteiro de Oliveira for welcoming us into your home and for your warm hospitality.

In Salvador: Thank you to Jorge Washington for showing us your Salvador and for cooking us the best ever *maxixada*! Thank you also to Dão, Tatiane, Sandra and Jamile.

In Cova da Onça: Thank you to Silvio da Conceição de Jesus for showing us how you make your incredible *azeite de dendê* and to Dora and América for your warmth, hospitality and all the delicious food.

In Minas Gerais: Thank you to Heloísa de Fátima Moutinho for welcoming us into your beautiful home like we were long-lost family and for cooking us the most spectacular Mineira feast!

Thank you to Wallace Lima for being our guide in Ouro Preto.

Thank you to my wonderful Tia Martha in Rio, what a joy it's been to see you so often over the last couple of years.

London

Thank you to Felicity Davis, whose talents know no bounds. From sourcing the beautiful props for the London shoot and designing the perfect set to testing and proofreading countless recipes, your input has been invaluable. Thank you for your vision and for being my trusted sounding board.

A huge thank you to Kim Lightbody for the beautiful recipe photography. You brought the dishes to life in a way that feels both vibrant and timeless. Your talent has been instrumental in shaping this book.

Thank you to Clare Cole for cooking all the food for the shoot with such care, speed and skill, and for being a calm and steady force amidst the whirlwind of each day. Thank you also for your invaluable assistance with the food styling. Thank you to Poppy Whittle, Martha Loving and Grace Jenkins for working with Clare to cook everything so beautifully and for bringing your vibrant, uplifting energy to the shoot.

To my beloved Beatriz Belfrage, thank you for your unwavering love and for being an incredibly caring big sis. You never cease to amaze me with your wisdom!

Thank you to my manager Nasuf Sherifi, an absolute legend in the game. I feel very lucky to be working with you.

Thank you to my brilliant agent Sabhbh Curran and to the team at Curtis Brown for all the support.

Thank you so much to Evi-O Studio for beautifully designing this book and bringing it to life.

Thank you to Melek Erdal, Marie Mitchell and Marina Garvey-Birch for your love and support.

To Max Déjardin, the very best addition to my life of late, thank you for being the sweetest and silliest partner in crime and my favorite person to eat with.

A massive and heartfelt thank you to the team at Ebury. To Liv Nightingall for her tireless work project managing this book and having to deal with my missed deadlines and neverending edits, I'm so grateful for your patience! Thank you to Celia Palazzo for commissioning this book. Thank you also to Stephanie Milner, Stephenie Reynolds, Catherine Ngwong, Margarida Mendes Ribeiro, Jaini Haria and Francesca Thomson for all your hard work bringing *FUSÃO* to life.

Nothing would make me happier than if this book inspires you to visit Brazil! If you do, please go and see the incredible contributors who make it so special.

Kenrick Lacruz
Amazon Extreme Tours
@kenricklacruz
www.amazonextremetours.com
Manaus, Amazonas

Jorge Washington
Culinária Musical
@culinariamusicalafrochefe
Salvador, Bahia

Heloísa de Fátima Moutinho
Pousada Recanto do Salto
@recantodosaltoof
Santo Antônio do Salto, Minas Gerais

Silvio da Conceição de Jesus
@silviododende
Cova da Onça, Bahia

First published in 2025 by

Interlink Books
An imprint of Interlink Publishing Group, Inc.
46 Crosby Street
Northampton, Massachusetts 01060
www.interlinkbooks.com

Published simultaneously in the United Kingdom by Ebury Press, part of the Penguin Random House group of companies.

Copyright © Ixta Belfrage 2025
Recipe photography © Kim Lightbody 2025
Brazil photography and recipe photography on pages 39, 51, 64, 121, 201, 207, 273, 275, 277 © Pedro Pinho 2025

All rights reserved. No part of this publication may be reproduced, stored in a retrieval system, or transmitted, in any form or by any means, electronic, mechanical, photocopying, recording or otherwise, without the prior written permission of the publishers.

Library of Congress Cataloging-in-Publication Data available
ISBN 978-1-62371-588-5

Editorial Director: Celia Palazzo
Senior Editor: Liv Nightingall
American Edition Editor: Leyla Moushabeck
Production Director: Catherine Ngwong
Copyeditor: Annie Lee
Design: Evi-O.Studio | Katherine Zhang
Typesetting: Evi-O.Studio | Katherine Zhang, Andrew Grune
Recipe Photographer: Kim Lightbody
Brazil Photographer: Pedro Pinho
Brazil Shoot Producer: Romã Nesi Pio
Set Designer: Felicity Davis
Food Stylist: Ixta Belfrage
Food Stylist Assistant: Clare Cole

Color origination by Altaimage Ltd.
Printed and bound in China by C&C Offset Printing Co., Ltd.

Interlink Publishing Group, Inc. is committed to a sustainable future for our business, our readers and our planet. This book is made from Forest Stewardship Council® certified paper.